Ethics Management in the Public Service

T0341159

Ethics Management in the Public Service offers a new perspective for ethics management in the Public Administration. The traditional approaches, relying on codified rules, regulations, and guidelines, have not yielded the results expected of them and have not managed to serve as an effective tool in the hands of public administrators struggling with ethical and moral questions. Unlike Code-based training strategies, focusing on the written word and its application in real-life situations, the authors introduce a sensory-based strategy to sharpen public administrators' senses. This type of training would first aim to help the public administrators become conscious of the use of their senses in a routine manner, not necessarily limited to ethical issues. Once an individual becomes more conscious of his or her acts and thinking process, they can better understand their motives, and again attempt to modify their conduct if and when necessary.

This book holds that sensory-based metaphors are an important device in applying the hermeneutic approach to ethics management in the public service, as they can enhance new understandings about the extent to which particular ethical principles might be disabling. Using metaphors as a management tool of public service ethics helps to communicate public values and ethical guidelines to public administrators.

Liza Ireni-Saban is Assistant Professor in the Lauder School of Government, Diplomacy and Strategy at the Interdisciplinary Center Herzliya, Israel.

Galit Berdugo is Head of Dean's Office in the Lauder School of Government, Diplomacy and Strategy at the Interdisciplinary Center Herzliya, Israel.

Routledge Critical Studies in Public Management

Edited by Stephen Osborne

For a full list of titles in this series, please visit www.routledge.com

The study and practice of public management has undergone profound changes across the world. Over the last quarter century, we have seen

- increasing criticism of public administration as the over-arching framework for the provision of public services,
- the rise (and critical appraisal) of the 'New Public Management' as an emergent paradigm for the provision of public services,
- the transformation of the 'public sector' into the cross-sectoral provision of public services, and
- the growth of the governance of inter-organizational relationships as an essential element in the provision of public services

In reality these trends have not so much replaced each other as elided or co-existed together—the public policy process has not gone away as a legitimate topic of study, intra-organizational management continues to be essential to the efficient provision of public services, whilst the governance of inter-organizational and inter-sectoral relationships is now essential to the effective provision of these services.

Further, whilst the study of public management has been enriched by contribution of a range of insights from the 'mainstream' management literature, it has also contributed to this literature in such areas as networks and inter-organizational collaboration, innovation, and stakeholder theory.

This series is dedicated to presenting and critiquing this important body of theory and empirical study. It will publish books that both explore and evaluate the emergent and developing nature of public administration, management and governance (in theory and practice) and examine the relationship with and contribution to the over-arching disciplines of management and organizational sociology.

Books in the series will be of interest to academics and researchers in this field, students undertaking advanced studies of it as part of their undergraduate or postgraduate degree and reflective policy makers and practitioners.

Ethics Management in the Public Service
A Sensory-based Strategy

Liza Ireni-Saban and Galit Berdugo

Routledge
Taylor & Francis Group
New York London

First published 2017 by Routledge

711 Third Avenue, New York, NY 10017
2 Park Square, Milton Park, Abingdon, Oxfordshire OX14 4RN

Routledge is an imprint of the Taylor & Francis Group, an informa business

First issued in paperback 2018

Library of Congress Cataloging in Publication Data
A catalog record has been requested for this book

ISBN: 978-1-138-11894-2 (hbk)
ISBN: 978-0-367-02660-8 (pbk)

Typeset in Sabon
by Apex CoVantage, LLC

Contents

Acknowledgments

We wish to thank some of the people who contributed to this book.

We would like to thank Professor Boaz Ganor, Dean of the Lauder School of Government, Diplomacy and Strategy at IDC Herzliya for his endless support and for being a source of inspiration. We also wish to thank the Lauder School's faculty and staff for their encouragement along the process of writing this book and for their friendship.

Many thanks to David Varley, commissioning editor of Routledge, for his constant support throughout this project. We would like to thank the manuscript's anonymous reviewers. They provided extremely constructive criticism that helped us to improve the quality of the manuscript. We also wish to thank Brianna Ascher and the production team at Routledge for their editorial assistance.

We are extremely grateful to Edna Oxman for her crucial editing and formatting assistance throughout the entire project. Edna has greatly contributed to the book, and we wish to convey our sincere thanks for her assistance.

On a personal note, we would like to thank our families: Varda and Alfred Ireni; Jacob Saban together with Amit, Lihi and Noya; and Esther Berdugo together with Liron, Pini and Avner. Without their unwavering support, love, patience and encouragement, this book would not exist.

This book is dedicated in memory of my father, Jacob Berdugo, who is greatly missed and loved. Thank you for setting the bar so high.

Introduction

"Red tape", "Bands of a mummy", "iron cage"—each of these metaphors were used for decades to conceal public administrators' failure to think and act effectively. Metaphors are assumed to function both negatively and positively. The power of metaphors lies in that they construct new ways of understanding, extend and even change popular attitudes. This is of particular value for studying public administration ethics because public administration has experienced a transformation of professional identity in the past thirty years. This book aims to shed light on the worldview of ethics management in the public service created through the use of sensory-based metaphors. In this book we wish to support ethics management practices to see more clearly how metaphors can positively shape and inspire public service ethics and could further do so in the twenty-first century.

One of the major challenges in today's increasingly complex and diverse work environment of public administrators is how the public service should manage and communicate its ethics and professional identity. Meeting the demands of various stakeholders such as governments, elected officials, and the public involves the exercise of discretionary judgment. This often presents great difficulty for public officials faced with the inherent conflict of commitments within the Public Administration.

In the past few years, there has been a proliferation of Codes of Ethics and Rules of Conduct that deal with ethics management in the public service. (Armstrong 2005; Ireni-Saban 2015; Menzel 2012) However, critics have argued that the trend of codification is illusory. Rules and ethical guidelines entrenched in codes can guide expectations governing the behavior of public servants, yet cannot prescribe exactly what should be done when ethical dilemmas arise. Rules and codes of ethics are for the most part indicative of prioritization of the professional principles and values relevant to official conduct. For example, the first principle articulated in the American Society for Public Administration's (ASPA) Code of Ethics is to "Promote the interest of the public and put service to the public above service to oneself". The code specifies the ethical guidelines behind the first principle as "to advance the good of the public as a whole, taking into account current and long-term interests of the society" (principle 1.a); "to exercise discretionary authority to promote the public interest" (principle 1.b); "to be prepared to make decisions that may not be popular but that are in the public's best interest" (principle 1.c); "to subordinate personal interests and institutional loyalties to the public good" (principle 1.d); and "to serve all persons with courtesy, respect, and dedication to high standards" (principle 1.e). (American Society for Public Administration March 2013)

Framed as such, public administrators need to promote the public interest, which often signifies a vague ideal that in some instances "refers to the outcomes best serving the long-run survival and well-being of a social collective construed as a public". (Bozeman 2007, 12) According to Bozeman, to pursue the public interest means "providing normative consensus about (a) the rights, benefits, and prerogatives to which citizens should (and should not) be entitled; (b) the obligations of citizens to society, the state, and one another; and (c) the principles on which governments and policies should be based." (Bozeman 2007, 13)

The question that remains is how exactly the code of ethics equips public administrators for right judgment and conduct when other public values may come into conflict with it, such as effectiveness or individual rights. (Stone 2012) Having the codes and ethical standards enables public administrators to feel part of a professional community that is often no more than an external and narrow concern in doing the right thing. Public officials will always need to follow rules and ethical guidelines; however, it is best to do so while being able to exert inner reasoning skills to develop their own judgment.

The ability to meaningfully reflect upon and act in the public interest involves the use of practical wisdom. Practical wisdom refers to the ability to perceive the salient features of particular situations, to have the appropriate emotions about them, to deliberate about what is appropriate in these situations by taking into account the particularities of practice situations, and to act in a responsible way. To do so, ethics management in the public service should go much further than just complying with existing rules and codes of ethics. It should deal with managing ethics as an ongoing process of building ethical competencies and professional identity for public officials.

Central to this capacity-building process is the idea that professional ethical competencies expected from public servants are aimed at developing a "proactive mindset", which encourages a spirit associated with adaptability to the dynamic and unstable nature of policy environments. This requires impartiality, communication skills, and entrepreneurial and innovative ability to meet the common good. (Lawton and Doig 2006) To better explore the potential for developing a strategy to enhance practical wisdom for public administrators, we take a step back to hermeneutics.

Philosophical hermeneutics is described as the voice of the other, while being aware of one's own bias. This requires "the skill of being critically distant while remaining involved, attentive, and caring towards the other". (Davey 2006, xvi) According to Gadamer (2006 [1975]), understanding takes place in every aspect of our experiences and is deeply intertwined in all human experience. In essence, Gadamer calls on the individual to situate oneself in the place of the other, by acknowledging the otherness of the other. (Gadamer 2006 [1975]) Thus, it is through this process that one gradually contributes to the other and is being contributed to by the prism of the other, creating a common understanding that serves as the basis for common growth. The process each individual is going through can be referred to as *Bildung*, a key concept in philosophical *hermeneutics*. (Gadamer 2006 [1975])

Bildung mainly represents one's "formation, cultivation and education" (Davey 2006, 37), which can be achieved through interaction with one's cultural, social, and geographical environment. (Kontje 1993) For Gadamer, *Bildung* is the individual's disposition that pursues an inner process of forming and cultivating the self as an intellectual and moral endeavor, while keeping oneself open to the other without sacrificing one's own past, biases, and particularities. Gadamer's hermeneutics provides insights into the very ethical reasoning process in which public administrators engage when tasked with managing ethical dilemmas and value conflicts. *Bildung* can be applied to situations where public administrators encounter values and ethical principles such as the public interest that are not easily understood and require some serious effort to reflect and act upon. That is to say, the public administrator is expected to follow the codified ethical standard while remaining open to reforming, open to meanings, and open to gaining insights into the public interests and understandings.

It is suggested that the philosophical grounding of hermeneutics enables analysis to move beyond the language of codes to the values and ideas behind them. Such transformation can be drawn on hermeneutically to make sense of ethics in the public service. (Balfour and Mesaros 1994)

This book holds that metaphors are an important device in applying the hermeneutic approach to ethics management in the public service, as they can enhance new understandings about the extent to which particular ethical principles might be disabling. Using metaphors as a management tool of public service ethics helps to communicate public values and ethical guidelines to public administrators. Treating metaphor as a research device may strike some as unusual. The study of metaphors is centered on what a metaphor is and how it works. According to Black (1955), it is through metaphors that we encounter the world, as they enable us to perceive and construct reality. This idea is pursued by Schön (1979, 254), who argues that metaphors are "central to the task of accounting for our perspectives on the world: how we think about things, make sense of reality, and set the problems we later try to solve". According to Schön, the importance of metaphors lies in their capacity "by which new perspectives on the world come into existence" (1979, 254) and, as such, pave the way for new understandings. In Reddy's (1979) study of the "conduit metaphor", metaphors are treated as a communication channel that transfers thoughts and emotions. Lakoff and Johnson (1980, 6) even extend this role of metaphors by noting that "linguistic expressions are possible precisely because there are metaphors in a person's conceptual system". As such, Lakoff and Johnson charge that metaphor "allows us to refer to it [a certain issue], quantify it, identify a particular aspect of it . . . and perhaps even believe that we understand it". (1980, 26)

While each of these scholars has put their own slant on the study of metaphors and how they work, they all concur in assigning them a heuristic device, for their capacity to allow new ways of understanding. For this capacity, the concept of metaphor that underlies the present work holds an intriguing promise for understanding the ways in which the hermeneutic approach to ethics management in the public service can be enhanced. One can assume that if values or ethical guidelines used by public officials are communicated through metaphors, then it is reasonable to believe that metaphors can open up new and multiple ways of understanding, which can be related to daily practices and in turn will be able to shed new light on how public administrators should view their professional identity and commitments.

As a source of metaphors, sensory experience is particularly rich. During recent years, the role of sensory experience in judging and deciding has gained much interest in marketing. A sensory-based strategy in marketing aims to use the unconscious sensory stimuli to reach the individual in a more intimate and personal way and engage customers and their behavior to create brand awareness and establish a sustainable image of a brand. (Krishna 2012; Waskul and Vannini 2008) A deeper and sustainable level of customers' overall experience can be realized through emotional linkages. Here, emotional linkage or experience involves the senses and feelings. To establish such imprints, sensory marketing desires to activate all five senses—smell, sound, sight, taste, and touch. The five senses are the focus of a company's marketing actions that emphasize the development and delivery of sensory experiences.

From a hermeneutic perspective, we consider the purpose of public service to be the creation and delivery of public value through communicative action that draws on sensory-emotional dynamics. Gadamer's notion of *Bildung* thus resonates tantalizingly with the idea of felt-sense as a way of knowing with and through the senses (Gendlin 1997 [1962], 1–5) to allow a clear space for listening and for unbiased dialogue. But how can the senses be drawn on hermeneutically to make sense and enable *Bildung* or understanding in the public service? It is suggested that metaphors arising from sensory experience may function as a mechanism for generating new understanding and, in turn, can progressively revise the pre-understanding/prejudice as referred to by Gadamer.

The Book's Outline

In Chapter 1 we provide a valuable and thoughtful understanding of ethics management in the public service. We discuss two main approaches to ethics management, namely Compliance-based and Integrity-based, also referred to as the Low-road and High-road approaches, respectively, or the "verification" vs. "values" set of integrity institutions. The chapter ends by outlining the need to integrate both approaches in pursuing a complete picture of professional ethics for public administrators. It is suggested that codification of professional conduct—as one component of ethics management—may contribute particularly to increased clarity about the ethical expectations of the professional association, whereas ethical reasoning and training may improve opportunities to identify ethical dilemmas and value conflicts that arise in daily practice.

Chapter 2 bridges the previous chapter and the subsequent chapters by developing a theoretical foundation that links ethics management in the public services with sensory-based strategies. For the delivery of public service to be effective, public servants need to feel, hear, and see the public in a metaphoric manner. To describe this task of understanding, this chapter addresses the philosophical thought of Hans-Georg Gadamer, which discerns the process of interpreting and understanding from someone else's perspective. We articulate Gadamer's work in relation to reading, understanding, and interpreting public management ethics.

Chapter 3 provides an overview of how metaphors work and enter into the composition of the political science discipline in general and public administration in particular. We then explore the implications for public administration ethics on claims that metaphors can facilitate new ways of understanding.

Chapter 4 draws on the synergies between Gadamer's notion of *Bildung* and sensory-based metaphors. The chapter provides a brief overview of metaphors and their hermeneutic relationship with understanding/*Bildung* and explores the implications for ethics management in the public service. The chapter places emphasis on the role of sensory experience as a source for metaphors engaged in a hermeneutical process of generating new understanding. More precisely, we investigate how sensual perception meets social, cultural, and moral order, thus compelling reflexive forms of sense-making by which people manage moral deliberation. Finally, we briefly expound on the application of sensory-based strategies in education and marketing.

In chapters 5 through 9, the applicability of sensory-based metaphors to ethics management is considered by exploring each of the senses while transcending their physical meaning onto a metaphoric meaning, taking into consideration their ethical reasoning significance. We draw on the five senses—sight, smell, hearing, touch, and taste. These senses are considered as reflections of administrators' daily lives, and by using them they are able to create a bond between themselves and their professional values and practice.

In Chapter 5 we investigate the moral sense of seeing, interpreted as the ability and the need for public servants to foresee the implications and consequences of public policies on the diverse layers of the population. Being the representatives of the public interest, public servants must "know their audience" and think strategically and flexibly when implementing policies of any sort and, if needed, bring the public's concerns to the attention of decision-makers.

Chapter 6 discerns the sense of hearing, interpreted as the obligation relative to public servants to remain attentive to their surroundings, by putting oneself in the place of the other. By internalizing the needs and requests of the public and truly listening to their voice, public servants will better communicate with their communities and be able to provide a better, more ethical and suitable public service.

Chapter 7 explores the way smell triggers personal and institutional memory, which is key for quality public service. It is vital for public servants to regard the broader perspective of their role and learn from personal and organizational experience as a means to ameliorate and gain professional excellence within the public service. Unlike political positions, public service positions are the backbone of the entire administration and are responsible for the stability of the democratic system. In that sense, the ability to "smell" and retain past policies is no less than critical in order to maintain the ability to govern and keep the democratic values in place.

Chapter 8 examines the way touch implies an active engagement with someone or something. It is in this respect that we encourage public servants to act dynamically and engage with the public, while, in turn, encouraging the public to play an active role in the public sphere. By reaching out to the public, the administration is applying New Public Management concepts according to which citizens ought not to be taken for granted and whose trust in the public administration must be acquired. Active engagement with the public and the sharing of public decisions and protocols will enhance the citizens' loyalty towards the administration and, in due course, also their trust.

Chapter 9 explores how the sense of taste is drawn metaphorically in public service ethics. Public servants, as representatives of the public interest, are tasked with acting tastefully, while applying their discretionary judgment and using their experience and expertise in the effort of making sensible decisions. Professional public servants have the added value of serving the public while playing a role in the central administration. It is therefore their role, within the limit of their authority and when necessary, to bridge these two worlds sensibly and tastefully.

Chapter 10 attempts to showcase how the five senses can and should be used in the practical realm of the Public Administration. We have chosen to focus on the ASPA Code of Ethics and implement its core principles in a sensory manner. We argue that sense-making highlights how the five human senses, i.e., sight, smell, hearing, touch, and taste, intersect with ethical discourse thus compelling reflexive forms of somatic work by which a bond can be created between them and public administrators' professional practice.

In the conclusion, we reflect on the value of using sensory-based metaphors used in ethics management in the public service, while calling for this innovative perspective to become inherent in the ethical decision-making process within the Public Administration. This can be achieved by ethical training based on synesthesia; that is, training public administrators to automatically "activate their senses" once an ethical issue is identified. This way, for instance, when the public's opinion is sought, the administrator will immediately proceed with actively reaching out to the public (sense of touch) while listening to their concerns (hearing), and applying his or her judgment (taste) in order to implement new policies.

Bibliography

American Society for Public Administration (ASPA). March 2013. "Code of Ethics." http://www.aspanet.org/PUBLIC/ASPADocs/ASPA%20Code%20of%20Ethics-2013%20with%20Practices.pdf

Armstrong, Elia. 2005. *Integrity, Transparency and Accountability in Public Administration: Recent Trends, Regional and International Developments and Emerging Issues*. New York: United Nations Department of Economic and Social Affairs.

Balfour, Danny L., and William Mesaros. 1994. "Connecting Local Narratives: Public Administration as a Hermeneutic Science." *Public Administration Review* 54.6:559–64.

Black, Max. 1955. "Metaphor." *Proceedings of the Aristotelian Society* 55:273–94.

Bozeman, Barry. 2007. *Public Values and Public Interest: Counterbalancing Economic Individualism*. Washington, DC: Georgetown University Press.

Davey, Nicholas. 2006. *Unquiet Understanding: Gadamer's Philosophical Hermeneutics*. Albany: State University of New York Press.

Gadamer, Hans-Georg. 2006 [1975]. *Truth and Method*, 2nd ed. New York: Continuum.

Gendlin, Eugene. 1997 [1962]. *Experiencing and the Creation of Meaning*. Evanston, IL: Northwestern University Press.

Ireni-Saban, Liza. 2015. "Understanding the Obligations of Codes of Ethics." In *Handbook of Public Administration*, 3rd ed., edited by James Perry and Rob Christensen, 597–615. San Francisco, CA: Jossey-Bass.

Kontje, Todd Curtis. 1993. *The German Bildungsroman: History of a National Genre*. Columbia, SC: Camden House.

Krishna, Aradhna. 2012. "An Integrative Review of Sensory Marketing: Engaging the Senses to Affect Perception, Judgment and Behavior." *Journal of Consumer Psychology* 22.3:332–51.

Lakoff, George, and Mark Johnson. 1980. *Metaphors We Live By*. Chicago: University of Chicago Press.

Lawton, Alan, and Alan Doig. 2006. "Researching Ethics for Public Service Organizations: The View from Europe." *Public Integrity* 8.1:11–34.

Menzel, Donald C. 2012. *Ethics Management for Public Administrators: Leading and Building Organizations of Integrity*, 2nd ed. Armonk, NY: M. E. Sharpe, Inc.

Reddy, Michael J. 1979. "The Conduit Metaphor." In *Metaphor and Thought*, edited by Andrew Ortony, 284–324. Cambridge, UK: Cambridge University Press.

Schön, Donald A. 1979. "Generative Metaphor: A Perspective on Problem-Setting in Social Policy." In *Metaphor and Thought*, edited by Andrew Ortony, 254–83. Cambridge, UK: Cambridge University Press.

Stone, Donald A. 2012. *Policy Paradox: The Art of Political Decision Making*, 3rd ed. New York: W. W. Norton and Company.

Waskul, Dennis D., and Phillip Vannini. 2008. "Smell, Odor, and Somatic Work: Sense-Making and Sensory Management." *Social Psychology Quarterly* 71:53–71.

1 Ethics Management in the Public Services

Ethics management is often defined as the process of applying ethics to organizational contexts, aiming at promoting ethical conduct and impeding unethical behavior. (Frederickson and Ghere 2005; Kaptein 1998; Menzel 2007; OECD 1996; OECD-PUMA 1998; Van Wart and Dicke 2008) The field of ethics management deals with the "systematic and coherent development of activities and the taking of measures in order to realize the fundamental justified expectations of stakeholders and to balance conflicting expectations of stakeholders in an adequate way". (Kaptein 1998, 42) Thus, management of ethics comprises shared values, beliefs, and expectations of members of an organization about how the organization encourages them to behave ethically and prevents them from behaving unethically. There are various tools available to manage ethics in organizations with which to promote the highest standard of professional conduct including ethics codes, ethics committees, ethics audits, ethics training, and other disciplinary measures for sanctioning unethical behavior and rewarding ethical behavior.

The revival of ethics in public service literature inevitably influences the debates about what counts as a "profession", since "profession" or "professional behavior" is often relatively narrowly defined as possession of certain key characteristics and values by an occupational group. In what follows we suggest that the professionals of the public sphere are rightfully held to a higher standard of ethics and are expected to maintain the public interest in each and every decision or action they take, or choose not to take. An important element of the rationale for ethics management in the public service could be said to be the provision of identifiable core values and norms that are recognized and manifested by the professionals in this field.

Professionalism in the Public Service

Ethics is generally defined as a "system or code of conduct based on universal moral duties and obligations which indicate how one should behave; it deals with the ability to distinguish good from evil, right from wrong and propriety from impropriety". (Josephson 1989, 2) Professionalism is viewed as a personal characteristic that is entrenched in an approach to an occupation that leads to a right action. Oakley and Cocking (2001, 100) argue that a good profession is one that must be perceived as an end in itself and be justified by reference to the "moral good which the proper performance of his or her professional role is supposed to serve". Such definition calls for professionals to serve some higher good—that is, a good that is associated with a human good. Professional ethics, according to Kasher, incorporates Oakley and Cocking's definition of professionalism that sustains purposive practices in terms of principles and rules to guide proper behavior that he labels the "practical idea of professional activity". (Kasher 2003) Following the general understanding of professionality, which can be seen when doctors properly aim for the health of their patients; lawyers, for legal justice for their clients; and teachers, for the education of their students—we may say that each of them performs professional acts within professional purposive practices. Although professional acts differ from each other in many respects, we use the label of "professional" for all of them. We arrive at the notion of professional practice or actions by identifying professions not with specific groups of people, but rather with certain professional practices. In other words, teaching is not only what teachers do; teachers are those people that engage in the professional practice of teaching.

Kasher's definition of professionalism (2005; Moataz 2011) suggests that professions have an ethics of their own, different from the morality of ethics of ordinary people or the general public, while restrained by norms and ideals of the wider community such as the basic norms of democracy. In a more configured manner, Kasher offers to view professional ethics as forming a "practical ideal" made of three concentric circles; the inner circle includes a series of values or a list of principles common to every profession or practice, the middle circle includes a series of values or a list of principles that guide a particular profession or a given practice, and the external circle incorporates social and universal values. The essence of professional practice is understood as a major aspect in identifying one profession as different from all others. For example, the medical and nursing professions are different, yet they appear to share values common to many professions such as the value of healing. They must be differentiated on the grounds of specific rules and principles in the pursuit of the patient's health. These principles and rules should spell out the nature of the professional practice of a given profession. Generally speaking, we need to put the notion of professional practice under philosophical scrutiny.

Professional ethics, then, can be evaluated properly only against a distinct context of action. In order to function in any professional area, each profession requires the knowledge and skills necessary for working toward the relevant purposive practices. For example, physicians must gain knowledge of anatomy and physiology and to prescribe medication because these tools are necessary to the pursuit of health. Lawyers must learn to prepare legal documents and master evidence and arguments to be presented in order to achieve legal justice for their client. The possession of appropriate knowledge and special skills brings the ability to solve ordinary and unexpected problems under certain circumstances of professional action. However, knowledge and skills alone are insufficient; within the context of action, skills alone do not possess any over-arching value commitment. Indeed, it would be confusing to try to define professions by skills because the same concrete skills may be used by different professions in pursuit of their own organizing values. What counts in terms of the definition of the profession is not so much what kinds of tools are directed towards particular ends and goods. For example, a physician is expected to have a concept of their area of professional activity, that is, to be able to understand the essence of medicine as a vocation. The scope, structure, and success or failure of the medical interventions by medical practitioners can be understood only in terms of the knowledge, skills, and underlying global understanding of healing that properly regulates that profession's activities. Such understanding leads to viewing the professional practice in the full honorific sense, in terms of basic values of that professional practice, and then to regulate such activity in terms of guiding principles and rules of behavior.

In this sense and drawing on the same context, public servants are expected to hold the knowledge and skills necessary in order to provide the public with a quality public service. This requires the understanding of both the theoretical and practical aspects of public service, whether this entails academic endeavors and professional experience at the same time. However, as knowledgeable and experienced the public servant would be, this cannot be sufficient. Public servants must also hold the same values, principles and basic beliefs as those placed in the forefront of the regime they serve. As this oeuvre would focus on democratic regimes, alone, all public servants of the matter must hold liberal and democratic notions at heart, while giving them life on a daily basis. The public servants' skill sets should therefore entail the ability to maintain the core values of the democratic society such as equality, freedom, and the rule of law. This while keeping the public interest as the first priority. The faculty of public servants to regard the "bigger picture" and favor the public interest at all times would allow them to provide the citizens with the best possible public service.

Drawing on this aspect we can view public servants as virtuous citizens and as guardians of community interests. Virtuous citizenship is a key requirement for the practice of democratic governance and administration. Commitment to democratic values, responsiveness, responsibility, and moral conduct are virtues of democratic citizenship. Thus, norms of civility, tolerance, and respect for equality and for citizens' rights and obligations are basic tenets in civil servants' professional ethics. (Ireni-Saban 2015) In October of 2009 the National Association of Schools of Public Affairs and Administration (NASPAA) issued a new set of accreditation standards for degree programs in public affairs and administration. The new standards contain desired public values and ethical principles of behavior to foster specific public service attitudes in students of public administration:

> NASPAA expects an accredited program to be explicit about the public service values to which it gives priority; to clarify the ways in which it embeds these values in its internal governance; and to demonstrate that its students learn the tools and competencies to apply and take these values into consideration in their professional activities.
>
> (NASPAA 2009, 4)

This reform indicates the current attention given to the employment of public values in the process of professional socialization in the field of public administration across academic and practitioners' discourses. Within the new NASPAA standards, public service values are grouped into four categories including include "*pursuing* the public interest with accountability and transparency" (democratic values); "*serving* professionally with competence, efficiency, and objectivity" (professional values); "*acting* ethically so as to uphold the public trust" (ethical values); and "*demonstrating* respect, equity, and fairness in dealings with citizens and fellow public servants" (human values). (2009, 2; emphasis added)

Approaches to Ethics Management in the Public Service

Ethics management in the public service rests on two main approaches, namely Compliance-based and Integrity-based, also referred to as the Low-road and High-road approaches, respectively, (Rohr 1978), or the "verification" vs. "values" set of integrity institutions. (Piotrowski 2014; Uhr 1999)

The **compliance or low-road approach** emphasizes the importance of imposing external controls on the behavior of civil servants. (For earlier discussion on the importance of imposing internal and external controls on public servants, see Cooper 1998, 131–63). Formal and comprehensive rules and procedures are designed to guide the decision-making process so that "the individual ethical choice is limited to choosing to follow the rules (ethical thing to do) or to violate them by commission or omission (unethical acts)". (Fox 2001, 110) The compliance approach identifies the ways in which the ethical position of the organization with regard to its commitments and the expectations placed on it is communicated to public administrators through the adoption of codes and the enforcement of ethical conduct. To improve ethical decision-making in public administration, ethics management can introduce an ethics program consisting of instruments such as legislation, codes of conduct and ethics, extensive enforcement mechanisms, and centralized control institutions with extensive authority. (Maesschalck 2004a)

Codes of Ethics, for example, are viewed as the explicit manifestation of a set of commitments taken on by the organization or profession to each of its members together with the basic values and norms that orient its activity.

We can only generate certain expectations if initially we are able to make known our commitments. For that, Codes of Ethics become an important management tool for building the ethical culture of a profession or organization by improving the profession's reputation and developing a deep sense of commitment to ethical behavior and pride among professional community members. (Ireni-Saban 2015)

Within public administration, codes of ethics are to be understood as an attempt to maintain public trust and confidence in the public sector. Codes of Ethics provide practical guidance for public servants on ethical behavior to enhance mutual understanding within the interaction between public administration and the community at large. According to Neil Brady: "Especially in the public sector, where issues are broad and complex, it should be clear that no single ethical perspective is adequate and no perspective should be neglected." (Brady 2003, 533) The common thread stated by Brady is that codifying ethical conduct in the public service demands that a professional individual become a practitioner who needs the help provided by the code to fully understand accepted values and standards in the realm of day-to-day practice. Effective implementation and communication of Codes of Ethics are likely to contribute to developing the professional identity of public administration that can maintain a positive reputation in the eyes of the public. The rationale behind the Code's implementation framework is that improved communication of professional identity may result in public officials having increased confidence and comfort, making ethical decisions based on clear understanding of their moral obligations and responsibilities to the public as part of their professional integrity. (Cooper 2004; Hejka-Ekins 1988; Maesschalck 2004b; Svara 2007; West and Berman 2004)

While codes of ethics in public administration aim at governing the public service, that is, to serve the public interests, they diverge across national and governmental settings.

In an effort to ensure the professional practice of public servants, the American Society for Public Administration (ASPA) established the first Code of Ethics in 1984. Svara reviews the background and the changes introduced by the codification process of the ASPA code. Svara points out how ASPA had moved from strict specificity towards control and enforcement by professional community members. (Winn in Menzel 2010, 123; Svara 2014) He shows that the broadened ASPA code can complement the more focused codes of other specialized associations of public officials and help administrators understand the full scope of responsibilities they have as public servants as well as their specific responsibilities as city managers, planners, social workers, police officers, or other categories of public service professionals. (Svara 2014) The 2013 code incorporates a broader set of ethical responsibilities that link professionalism with moral reasoning in a way that enables public officials to draw the connection between work-related specific responsibilities and the more shared and generalized issue of public service. (Svara 2014)

Comparative Approach to Ethics Management

In the United Kingdom, the Civil Service Code was set to promote civil service management reforms. The Code, published in 1996, includes a set of core civil service values and the standards of behavior expected of all civil servants, including:

> Integrity—putting the obligations of public service above personal interests; Honesty—being truthful and open; Objectivity—basing advice and decisions on rigorous analysis of the evidence; and Impartiality—acting solely according to the merits of the case and serving governments of different political parties equally well.
>
> (Civil Service Code 1996)

Among the Baltic countries, Estonia was the first to introduce a Public Service Code of Ethics, which was integrated into the Public Service Act in 1999. The first article of the Estonian Code concentrates on the idea that public administrators have an obligation to support government reforms of democratic public management. The Code articulates the new image of the public servant who has responsibilities to both political supervisors and to citizens and is required to balance the two: "An official is a citizen in the service of people." The democratic values entrenched in the Code include "Serving the public, respect for the law and people, loyalty to government, public participation, political neutrality, impartiality, objectivity, predictability, openness, honesty, reliability, responsibility, consciousness, competence." (Public Service Code of Ethics (Estonia) 1999)

In China, the 1993 civil service managerial reform increased the value of ethical deliberation in performing official duties. The Chinese government codified civil service processes and structures and finally initiated the Norms of Behavior and Professional Ethics of State Civil Servants (*Guojia gongwuyuan xingwei guifan*) in 2002. The codification process has signaled a growing commitment to impart professionalism and political accountability among Chinese civil servants. (Tsao and Worthley 2009) In 2011, the Chinese government developed an ethics training program for the country's civil servants to enhance values of responsibility and accountability to citizens. (Huazhong 2011)

The purpose of the Macedonian Code of Ethics for Civil Service is to "regulate the manner of conduct and the operations of the civil servants in order to ensure recognition of the principles of legality, professional integrity, efficiency and loyalty in performing their official duties." (Agency for Administration of the Republic of Macedonia 2002) The code of ethics was part of new reforms introduced in the public administration of Macedonia during the first decade of the twenty-first century. These reforms were initiated to educate those civil servants with low performance and unethical behavior in their daily encounter with the citizens. (Selami 2012)

In both the Chinese and Macedonian cases, the underlying assumption behind the introduction of Codes to support public servants' socialization is that the institutional context of the public service has an over-riding influence on the moral decisions of professional public servants, rather than individuals' ability to make ethical judgments. (Ireni-Saban 2015)

In Canada, the Values and Ethics Code for the Public Sector came into force on April 2, 2012. The Code has the purpose to improve the reputation of public service by complying with principles of equal treatment, effectiveness, integrity, and accountability when performing their duties. (The Values and Ethics Code for the Public Sector 2012)

In Poland, the purpose of the Civil Service Code of Ethics (2003) is specified as follows: "To increase the citizen's confidence in the State and its authorities." This is also embedded in the Code of the Czech Republic (2004), which seeks "to gain and maintain the public trust, to promote the desired standards of behaviour among public servants and to inform the public about the standards that citizens have a right to demand from public administration employees." (Code of Ethics of Public Servants Czech Republic 2004) The Code of Ethics was initiated by the Czech Republic authorities with the purpose of monitoring citizens' attitudes towards government and the public administration due to growing levels of citizens' distrust in the public service.

The need to raise public trust in public administration is entrenched in the Finnish Code (Finland Ministry of Finance 2005):

> In our own work, we safeguard the trustworthiness of public service, so that citizens' trust in the impartiality and independence of public service activities is preserved. We discharge our duties in compliance with legislation and principles of good administrative practice. Our operation must also be seen to fulfil the requirements of good administrative practice in the eyes of an external evaluator.[1]

The importance of raising public trust through the codification of ethical behavior in the public service is also recognized in the Asian context. Both Japan and South Korea became aware of the need to enhance public trust in government and increase effective communication with citizens. (Kim 2010) This act was part of the government's efforts to undermine the dominance of Confucian tradition and values and in this way to strengthen the legitimacy of public service in the eyes of the citizens. (Mishler and Rose 2001)

However, despite the increasing use of codes of ethics across national and institutional settings, there is relatively little empirical evidence regarding their effectiveness on ethical decision-making and behavior in public administrations. The majority of studies treat the theoretical utility of codes of ethics in the public service, and most studies tend to agree that the theoretical utility lies in sending significant messages about the organization's expectations of ethical conduct. However, in the literature there appears to be no agreement as to whether codes of ethics are useful and effective in enhancing ethical decision-making or conduct in the public service. (Frederickson and Ghere 2005; Gueras and Garofalo 2005; Lawton and Doig 2005–2006; Maesschalck 2004b; Menzel 2005, 2010)

Effectiveness of Codes of Ethics

Kaptein and Schwartz (2008) identified a relatively small number of studies (79) examining the behavioral effects of codes of ethics in private organizations, studies that yielded mixed results. This joins Pelletier and Bligh's critique (2006), according to which codes of ethics in private organizations may present a formal set of desired values and ethical standards; however, they cannot be implemented without the support of the informal framework that consists of the attitudes and behaviors perceived by the employees. Therefore, deliberations within the organization regarding ethical issues, the establishment of ethical decision-making procedures, or the exemplification of noteworthy ethical behavior may influence the degree to which employees perceive the compliance between the code of the ethics and the expected line of conduct. Thus, the researchers conclude that one of the primary reasons for inconsistency between codes of ethics and practical conduct lies "in the congruence (or lack thereof) between formal and informal ethics codes". (Pelletier and Bligh 2006, 363)

Several studies have been conducted by Bowman and his colleagues since 1989 on ethics in public agencies with an emphasis on the effects of the ASPA Code of Ethics. (Bowman 1990; Bowman and Knox 2008; Bowman and Williams 1997) These studies focus on three key variables considered indicative of the effectiveness of the ASPA Code of Ethics: awareness of the code among public servants, its acceptability, and its enforceability within the public administration. The findings of these studies indicate a gradual awareness among public servants of the code, going from a poor acquaintance with it (in 1990 over 40 percent admit they have none) to 83 percent affirming familiarity with the code in 2008, presenting a real potential for it to impact daily management of public affairs. The studies go on to indicate a progressive acceptability and enforceability of the code, where the vast majority of the research body in 1990 admits the code is seldom used, while 62 percent claimed to use the code and its standards at work in 2008.

It is important to note, however, that in order for the code to be fully or more effectively implemented in the public service, the majority of the responders to all three surveys have emphasized that more customized policies are needed to accommodate the various needs of public administration workplaces. (Bowman and Knox 2008) That is to say, that although a gradual increase in the awareness and effectiveness of the ASPA Code of Ethics can be identified throughout the years, it presents a general framework for ethical conduct that is indifferent to specific traits relative to various public organizations and to the significantly distinctive requirements and realities public organizations are faced with.

Moreover, as pointed out by Sossin and Smith (2003), ethical codes and ethical guidelines in the public sphere are frequently viewed as "soft laws" whose enforcement is maintained merely by an independent auditor or an ethics committee whose authority is unclear. Therefore, any infringement of the theoretical ethical guidelines or the potential lack of consistency between the code of ethics and the actual conduct becomes tangible and might undermine the code's authority in the eyes of public servants, public organizations, and the general community.

A more recent study on measuring the effectiveness of codes of ethics was conducted across 154 national administrations relating to the effect of the code on the level of State corruption. The researchers concluded that having a code of ethics has no effect on corruption problems in the public context in both developed and developing countries. This being said, the primordial factor influencing the level of corruption was found to be the level of education in the country, distancing the code of ethics even further from its goal to diminish unethical state-run conduct. (Garcia-Sanchez, Rodriguez-Dominguez, and Gallego-Alvarez 2011)

The integrity or high-road approach encourages ethical behavior in the public service based on inner qualities including a person's moral character, moral judgment, and motives. (Stazyki and Davis 2015) Hejka-Ekins (2001) suggests that the moral judgment of an individual civil servant can be strengthened by cultivating the necessary values and norms, as well as by developing the skills in ethical decision-making needed to apply those values in daily work situations. Viewing ethics management through the lens of an integrity-based approach provides a different perspective for defining moral character, which encompasses both knowledge of the "right" thing to do and action to do what is good: "Relying on moral character, this route counts on ethical managers individually to reflect, decide, and act. Individual responsibility is both a starting and an end point on the integrity route in public service." (Lewis and Gilman 2012, 16–17) Moral character can be achieved through interactive training sessions, workshops, and individual coaching. (Bowman and Menzel 1998; Cooper and Menzel 2013; Lewis and Gilman 2012; Menzel 2007; Svara 2007)

Other normative investigations into the ways of applying an integrity-based approach in public administration practice concerns the employment of elements of practical wisdom. Practical Wisdom or, as Aristotle would call it, *phronesis*, is considered to be the Master Virtue that is essential for orchestrating all the other virtues. (Schwartz and Sharpe 2006) Aristotle defines *phronesis* as "the capacity of deliberating well about what is good and advantageous for oneself", and this is "what sort of thing contributes to the good life in general". (Aristotle 1962, Book VI, chapter 5, 1140a, lines 26–8) It is the trait or combination of traits that will allow the person to do the right thing in the right way and at the right time. (Bradshaw 2009) Certainly laws, rules, and regulations assist the person to make the right decision and act in a way that is most adequate; however, and most certainly in matters of ethical consideration, rules or codes are no substitute for Practical Wisdom, which should be inherent.

The Philosophy of Practical Wisdom

A great deal of insight into integrity or the high-road approach to ethics management in the public service, particularly in the sphere of professional ethics, can be gleaned from retracing our discussion of Greek philosophical roots of practical wisdom, particularly the insights gained from Aristotle's and Plato's concepts of virtue (*arete*), which can deepen the integrity approach to ethics management.

Arete, the Greek notion of virtue, denotes excellence in quality that is very much linked to well-functioning. Aristotle specified three types of human excellence (virtue) including bodily excellence, excellence of character (moral virtue), and excellence of intelligence (intellectual virtue). (Urmson 1998)

In Greek ethics, moral virtues or excellence of character refer to characteristics such as courage, temperance, and justice. Intellectual virtues encompass wisdom, which includes excellence in theoretical matters and practical wisdom (termed *phronesis* or prudence). Practical wisdom indicates excellence in practical affairs, and involves the ability to plan one's life well. (Urmson 1998) Viewed in this way, the intellectual virtue of practical wisdom (prudence) cannot be separable from moral virtue. (MacIntyre 1985, ch. 10–12; Urmson 1998)

Socrates's philosophy may provide a starting point for earlier discussion of practical wisdom theory. For Socrates, love, character, harmony, beauty, and truth are crucial to wisdom. (Birren and Svensson 2005; Robinson 1990) Socrates considers wisdom to function as an evolutionary tool in terms of thought and behavior that contributes to the adaptation and survival of communities. To maintain such function for the long term, Socrates argues that wisdom is needed to exercise the power of both practical and political purposes to bring about well-being. (Sherman 1997, 8–9) Government must build expertise and exercise knowledge and good judgment for the sake of society. (Osbeck and Robinson 2005)

Similarly, Plato views wisdom as a process of moral deliberation guided by the appropriate balancing of the three parts of the "soul"—that is, desire, spirit, and reason; such capacity is central for wisdom because it maintains harmony between the components of the soul. Wisdom for both Socrates and Plato fits then into moral deliberation and ethical conduct because it provides good judgment leading to good action.

Practical wisdom leads to excellence in ethical deliberation and therefore is a subject of ethics education so that professionals will be able to make sound ethical judgments in practice. According to Aristotle: "It is impossible to be good in the full sense of the word without practical wisdom or to be a man of practical wisdom without moral excellence or virtue." (1962, Book VI, chapter 13, 1144b, lines 31–2) For that, Aristotle puts an emphasis on the role of the educator and on the way people can develop moral expertise. It should be noted that viewing virtue as a skill requires different teaching tools that go beyond that which is needed for theoretical wisdom. Teaching practical wisdom and excellence of character should be grounded in everyday practice and cultivated by exemplary practitioners who acquired practical wisdom through years of experience. As articulated by Aristotle:

> We may grasp the nature of prudence [*phronesis*] if we consider what sort of people we call prudent. Well, it is thought to be the mark of a prudent man to be able to deliberate rightly about what is good and advantageous . . . But nobody deliberates about things that are invariable . . . So . . . prudence cannot be a science or art; not science [*episteme*] because what can be done is a variable (it may be done in different ways, or not done at all), and not art [*techne*] because action and production are generically different.
>
> For production aims at an end other than itself; but this is impossible in the case of action, because the end is merely doing *well*. What remains, then, is that it is a true state, reasoned, and capable of action with regard to things that are good or bad for man . . . We consider that this quality belongs to those who understand the management of households or states.
>
> (Book VI, chapter 5, 1140a, lines 1–23; italics in the original)

Ethics education cannot simply be concerned with teaching ethical roles and principles of ethical behavior but rather developing critical reflection by being able to identify moral dilemmas, to interpret situations, and to act wisely in relation to them. Such an approach to teaching practical wisdom is summarized by Urmson (1998, 26):

> Aristotle compares acquiring a good character with acquiring a skill. Paradoxical though it may sound, one learns to play the piano by playing the piano, and to ride a bicycle by riding one. Before one has acquired the art or skill one acts in accordance with the instructions of a teacher, who tells us what to do and one does it with effort. Gradually, by practice and repetition, it becomes effortless and second nature. In the same way, one is trained as a child (if lucky in one's parents and teachers) to become truthful, generous, fair and the like by being told how to behave well and encouraged to do so. Parents supply the intelligence and experience that one has not yet developed, and with practice and repetition it becomes easier and easier to follow their counsel . . . At the same time, he [Aristotle] believes, one's practical intelligence will develop so that one will less and less need parents and guardians to tell one how to

behave in various circumstances; one will come to see for oneself . . . If properly trained one comes to enjoy doing things the right way, to want to do things the right way, and to be distressed by doing things wrongly.

Practical Wisdom Applied in the Public Service

Rooney and McKenna (2008, 713) argue that developing Practical Wisdom in public administration involves an intellectual grasp of insight into the daily practices of public administrators, achieved through the process of introspection: "many of the ideas dealt with in public administration are complex or abstract, they require sensitive and good judgment and intuition if excellent public service outcomes are to be achieved" (Rooney and McKenna, 2008, 714). While knowledge and intellectual labor remain important aspects of the daily conduct of public administrators, one must review their role from a broader perspective, highlighting Practical Wisdom to include emotional sensitivity and moral judgment. Practical wisdom in the public service demonstrates particularly the things that cannot or are extremely difficult to teach or to be taught, but rather are inner abilities and are a product of one's background and personal character. This, in our eyes, is especially pertinent with regard to the ethical decision-making process of public administrators.

There are seven elements of wisdom common in ethics management literature including high level of consciousness, power of choice, internal locus of control, awareness of self-fulfilling prophecy, inclusiveness, abundance, and a decision-making process that is guided by honesty, logic, and reasonableness (Jones 2005):

- *High level of consciousness* means becoming aware of one's conduct, intentions, and obligations through introspection. (Rothberg 1993)
- *Power of choice* refers to the ability of people to use good judgment in determining actions and consideration of others who will be affected by these actions. (Maxwell 1984)
- *Internal locus of control* refers to the extent to which individuals realize that they possess means of control in response to circumstance and events and hold themselves responsible for their choices and actions. (Rotter 1966)
- *Awareness of self-fulfilling prophecy* involves how individuals may react to a particular situation in the way they perceive it and look for relevant information that confirms their perception regardless of what the situation means in reality. (Snow 1994)
- *Inclusiveness* refers to the extent to which people from diverse backgrounds or communities seek cooperation and promote fairness and equity.
- *Abundance* denotes positive qualities that impact on the development of a person's belief that there is always enough to meet the needs of all.

- Decision-making process that is guided by *honesty, logic, and reasonableness* allows individuals to live in harmony and have faith in doing the right thing.

While the Compliance and the Integrity approaches may seem to belong to opposite poles of management, they need not contradict each other, and in practice best ought to be used in combination, complementing and reinforcing desired behaviors. (Fox 2001) Indeed, a recent conceptual trend seems to favor bypassing these two approaches' distinctions and instead focusing on an integrative approach, taking into account several models of leadership in organizations.

Clearly, each approach of ethics management for public administration has the potential to shape the professional conduct of the public service. It is also conceivable that the individual approaches have a different relationship in terms of impact, strength, and nature with the professional ethics of civil servants. However, if mechanisms that can readily be communicated externally such as codes of ethics and integrity and the subjectivity of individual public servants are related to each other as multidimensional constructs, ethics management may be extended beyond knowledge of ethical guidelines and also depend on the integrity and subjectivity of individual public servants. For example, codification of professional conduct—as one component of ethics management—may contribute particularly to increased clarity about the ethical expectations of the professional association, whereas integrity ethical training may improve opportunities to discuss ethical dilemmas and ethical issues that arise in daily practice.

Viewed in this way, ethics management for public administration must attend to subjective and relational contexts just as much as to the regulation or codification of professional conduct. The role of a public administrator at this point is not as a detached observer of the ethical decision-making process but as an active participant in a relationship. Thus, the public administrator's way of relating, his or her conception of self, of others, and the world all directly impinge—for good or bad—on the process of responding ethically.

The question remains of how to cultivate the moral character as well as professional development that constitute ethical public service. According to Callahan (1980), there are five principles that should guide professional ethics training: stimulating the moral imagination; recognizing ethical issues; eliciting a sense of moral obligation; developing analytical skills; and tolerating and reducing disagreement and ambiguity. Although these guidelines were originally developed in the context of teaching ethics in higher education, they will be discussed here in the context of sensory-based strategies that can contribute to the realization of Callahan's principles at many levels of public service.

It is suggested that the philosophical grounding of hermeneutics enables analysis to move beyond the language of codes to the values and ideas behind them. Such transformation can be drawn on hermeneutically to make sense of ethics in the public service. (Balfour and Mesaros 1994) It is suggested that engaging with metaphors in a hermeneutic process can enable new understandings to emerge about the extent to which particular ethical principles in use might be disabling. As a source of metaphors, sensory experience is particularly rich. When employing hermeneutics, the purpose of public service is clearly seen as the creation and delivery of public value through communicative action that draws on sensory-emotional dynamics.

Note

1. Values in the Daily Job—Civil Servant's Ethics. A Handbook for the State Administration at http://workspace.unpan.org/sites/internet/documents/UNPAN91843. pdf (p.11)

Bibliography

Agency for Administration of the Republic of Macedonia. Code of Ethics for Civil Servants. 2002. http://www.aa.mk/WBStorage/Files/01_96_Eticcki_Kodeks.pdf

Aristotle. 1962. *Nicomachean Ethics*. Translated by Martin Ostwald. New York: Macmillan.

Balfour, Danny L., and William Mesaros. 1994. "Connecting Local Narratives: Public Administration as a Hermeneutic Science." *Public Administration Review* 54.6:559–64.

Birren, James E., and Cheryl M. Svensson. 2005. "Wisdom in History." In *A Handbook of Wisdom: Psychological Perspectives*, edited by Robert J. Sternberg and Jennifer Jordan, 3–31. Cambridge: Cambridge University Press.

Bowman, James S. 1990. "Ethics in Government: A National Survey of Public Administrators." *Public Administration Review* 50:345–53.

———, and Claire Connolly Knox. 2008. "Ethics in Government: No Matter How Long and Dark the Night." *Public Administration Review* 68:627–39.

———, and Donald C. Menzel, eds. 1998. *Teaching Ethics and Values in Public Administration Programs*. Albany, NY: SUNY Press.

———, and Russell L. Williams. 1997. "Ethics in Government: From a Winter of Despair to a Spring of Hope." *Public Administration Review* 57:517–26.

Bradshaw, John. 2009. *Reclaiming Virtue: How We Can Develop the Moral Intelligence to Do the Right Thing at the Right Time for the Right Reason*. Chicago: Bantam.

Brady, F. Neil. 2003. "Public Administration and the Ethics of Particularity." *Public Administration Review* 63:525–34.

Callahan, Daniel. 1980. "Goals in the Teaching of Ethics." In *Ethics in Teaching in Higher Education*, edited by Daniel Callahan and Sissela Bok, 61–80. New York: Plenus Press.

Civil Service Code (United Kingdom). 1996. http://www.civilservice.gov.uk/about/values

Civil Service Code of Ethics (Poland). 2003. http://www.osi.hu/lgi/publications/dp/html/08.html (2003.04.05).

Code of Ethics of Public Servants (Czech Republic). 2004. http://www.oecd.org/puma/ethics/events.htm (2002.04.12).

Cooper, Terry. 1998. *The Responsible Administrator*. San Francisco, CA: Jossey-Bass Publisher.

———. 2004. "Big Questions in Administrative Ethics: A Need for Focused, Collaborative Effort." *Public Administration Review* 64:395–407.

———, and Donald Menzel, eds. 2013. *Achieving Ethical Competence for Public Service Leadership*. Armonk, NY: M. E. Sharpe.

Finland Ministry of Finance. 2005. *Values in the Daily Job—Civil Servant's Ethics: A Handbook for the State Administration*,11. http://workspace.unpan.org/sites/internet/documents/UNPAN91843.pdf

Fox, Charles J. 2001. "The Use of Philosophy in Administrative Ethics." In *Handbook of Administrative Ethics*, edited by Terry L. Cooper, 105–30. New York: Marcel Dekker.

Frederickson, George H., and Richard K. Ghere. 2005. *Ethics in Public Management*. Armonk, NY: M. E. Sharpe.

Garcia-Sanchez, Isabel Maria, Luis Rodriguez-Dominguez, and Isabel Gallego-Alvarez. 2011. "Effectiveness of Ethics Codes in the Public Sphere: Are They Useful in Controlling Corruption?" *International Journal of Public Administration* 34:190–5.

Gueras, Dean, and Charles Garofalo. 2005. *Practical Ethics in Public Administration*, 2nd ed. Vienna, VA: Management Concepts.

Hejka-Ekins, April. 1988. "Teaching Ethics in Public Administration." *Public Administration Review* 47:885–91.

———. 2001. "Ethics in In-Service Training." In *Handbook of Administrative Ethics*, edited by Terry L. Cooper, 79–104. New York: Marcel Dekker.

Huazhong, Wang. 2011. "Civil Servants to be Taught Ethical Behavior." *China Daily*, November 7, 2011. http://www.deccanherald.com/content/202153/civil-servants-china-get-ethics.html

Ireni-Saban, Liza. 2015. "Understanding the Obligations of Codes of Ethics." In *Handbook of Public Administration*, 3rd ed., edited by James Perry and Rob Christensen, 598–615. San Francisco, CA: Jossey-Bass.

Jones, Coy A. 2005. "Wisdom Paradigms for the Enhancement of Ethical and Profitable Business Practices." *Journal of Business Ethics* 57:363–75.

Josephson, Michael. 1989. *Power, Politics and Ethics: Ethical Obligations and Opportunities of Government Service*. Marina del Rey, CA: Government Ethics Center, The Joseph & Edna Institute for the Advancement of Ethics.

Kaptein, Muel. 1998. *Ethics Management: Auditing and Developing the Ethical Content of Organizations*. Dordrecht: Kluwer Academic Publishers.

———, and Mark S. Schwartz. 2008. "The Effectiveness of Business Codes: A Critical Examination of Existing Studies and the Development of an Integrated Research Model." *Journal of Business Ethics* 77:111–27.

Kasher, Asa. 2003. "Professional Ethics." In *Ethical Issues in Mental Health Consultation and Therapy*, edited by Gabi Scheffler, Yehudit Achmon, and Gabriel Weil, 15–29. Jerusalem: Y. I. Magnes Publications [Hebrew].

———. 2005. "Professional Ethics and Collective Professional Autonomy: A Conceptual Analysis." *Ethical Perspectives* 12:67–97.

Kim, Soonhee. 2010. "Public Trust in Government in Japan and South Korea: Does the Rise of Critical Citizens Matter?" *Public Administration Review* 70:801–10.

Lawton, Alan, and Alan Doig. 2005–2006. "Researching Ethics for Public Service Organizations: The View from Europe." *Public Integrity* 8:11–34.

Lewis, Carol W., and Stuart C. Gilman. 2012. *The Ethics Challenge in Public Service.* San Francisco, CA: Jossey-Bass.

MacIntyre, Alasdair. 1985. *After Virtue: A Study in Moral Theory*, 2nd ed. London: Duckworth.

Maesschalck, Jerden. 2004a. "Approaches to Ethics Management in the Public Sector: A Proposed Extension of the Compliance-Integrity Continuum." *Public Integrity* 7:20–41.

———. 2004b. "The Impact of New Public Management Reforms on Public Servants' Ethics: Towards a Theory." *Public Administration* 82:465–89.

Maxwell, Nicholas. 1984. *From Knowledge to Wisdom.* Oxford: Blackwell.

Menzel, Donald C. 2005. "Research on Ethics and Integrity in Governance." *Public Integrity* 7:147–68.

———. 2007. *Ethics Management for Public Administrators: Building Organizations of Integrity.* New York: M. E. Sharpe.

———. 2010. *Ethical Moments in Government: Cases and Controversies.* Boca Raton, FL: CRC Press.

Mishler, William, and Richard Rose. 2001. "What Are the Origins of Political Trust? Testing Institutional and Cultural Theories in Post-Communist Societies." *Comparative Political Studies* 34:30–62.

Moataz, Fattah. 2011. "Professional Ethics and Public Administration in the United States." *International Journal of Public Administration* 34:65–72.

National Association of Schools of Public Affairs and Administration. 16 October 2009. "Accreditation Standards for Master's Degree Programs." http://www.naspaa.org/accreditation/doc/NS2009FinalVote10.16.2009.pdf

Oakley, Justin, and Dean Cocking. 2001. *Virtue Ethics and Professional Roles.* Cambridge: Cambridge University Press.

OECD. 1996. *Ethics in the Public Service: Current Issues and Practices.* Paris: Organisation for Economic Cooperation and Development.

OECD-PUMA. 1998. "Managing Ethics: An OECD Recommendation." *Focus: Public Management Gazette* 9:1–8. http://www.oecd.org/gov/publicsectorinnovation ande-government/1900037.pdf

Osbeck, Lisa M., and Daniel N. Robinson. 2005. "Philosophical Theories of Wisdom." In *A Handbook of Wisdom: Psychological Perspectives*, edited by Robert J. Sternberg and Jennifer Jordan, 61–83. Cambridge: Cambridge University Press.

Pelletier, Kathie L., and Michelle C. Bligh. 2006. "Rebounding from Corruption: Perceptions of Ethics Program Effectiveness in a Public Sector Organization." *Journal of Business Ethics* 67:359–74.

Piotrowski, Suzanne J. 2014. "Transparency: A Regime Value Linked With Ethics." *Administration & Society* 46:181–9.

Public Service Code of Ethics (Estonia). 1999. http://workspace.unpan.org/sites/internet/Documents/UNPAN038382.pdf

Robinson, Daniel N. 1990. "Wisdom through the Ages." In *Wisdom: Its Nature, Origins, and Development*, edited by Robert J. Sternberg, 13–24. Cambridge: Cambridge University Press.

Rohr, John. 1978. *Ethics for Bureaucrats.* New York: Marcel Dekker.

Rooney, David, and Bernard McKenna. 2008. "Wisdom in Public Administration: Looking for a Sociology of Wise Practice." *Public Administration Review* 68.4: 709–21.

Rothberg, Donald. 1993. "The Crisis of Modernity and the Emergence of Socially Engaged Spirituality." *Revision* 75:105–14.

Rotter, Julian B. 1966. "Generalized Expectancies for Internal versus External Control of Reinforcements." *Psychological Monographs* 80:1–28.

Schwartz, Barry, and Kenneth E. Sharpe. 2006. "Practical Wisdom: Aristotle Meets Positive Psychology." *Journal of Happiness Studies* 7:377–95.

Selami, Agim. 2012. "Quality of Public Service Delivery in the Civil Service of Macedonia: What Role for the Code of Ethics?" *Innovative Issues and Approaches in Social Sciences* 5:51–7.

Sherman, Nancy. 1997. *Making a Necessity of Virtue: Aristotle and Kant on Virtue.* Cambridge: Cambridge University Press.

Snow, Richard E. 1994. "Pygmalion and Intelligence?" *Current Directions in Psychological Science* 4:169–71.

Sossin, Lorne, and Charles W. Smith. 2003. "Hard Choices and Soft Law: Ethical Codes, Policy Guidelines and the Role of the Courts in Regulating Government." *Alberta Law Review* 40:867–93.

Stazyki, Edmund C., and Randall S. Davis. 2015. "Taking the 'High Road': Does Public Service Motivation Alter Ethical Decision Making Processes?" *Public Administration* 93(3): 627–45. First published online: 12 February 2015. doi:10.1111/padm.12158

Svara, James H. 2007. *The Ethics Primer for Public Administrators in Government and Nonprofit Organizations.* Sudbury, MA: Jones & Bartlett.

———. 2014. "Who Are the Keepers of the Code? Articulating and Upholding Ethical Standards in the Field of Public Administration." *Public Administration Review* 74:561–9.

Tsao, King Kwan, and John Abbott Worthley. 2009. "Civil Service Development in China and America: A Comparative Perspective." *Public Administration Review* 69:88–94.

Uhr, John. 1999. "Institutions of Integrity: Balancing Values and Verification in Democratic Government." *Public Integrity* 1:94–106.

Urmson, James O. 1998. *Aristotle's Ethics.* Oxford: Blackwell.

The Values and Ethics Code for the Public Sector (Canada). 2012. http://www.tbs-sct.gc.ca/chro-dprh/ve-eng.asp

Van Wart, Montgomery, and Lisa A. Dicke. 2008. *Administrative Leadership in the Public Sector.* New York: M. E. Sharpe.

West, Jonathan P., and Evan M. Berman. 2004. "Ethics Training in U.S. Cities: Content, Pedagogy, and Impact." *Public Integrity* 6:189–206.

2 *Bildung*

Gadamer's Hermeneutics and Ethics Management in the Public Service

The present chapter attempts to bridge the previous chapter and subsequent chapters by developing a theoretical foundation that links ethics management in the public services with sensory-based strategies. For the delivery of public service to be effective, public servants need to feel, hear, and see the public in a metaphoric manner. To describe this task of understanding, this chapter addresses the philosophical thought of Hans-Georg Gadamer, which discerns the process of interpreting and understanding from someone else's perspective. We articulate Gadamer's work in relation to reading, understanding, and interpreting public management ethics.

In the past few years, there has been a revival of grand theories of political philosophy, ethics, and socio-culture that have been applied to public administration theory: political philosophy (Aristotle, Kant, Marx, Hobbes, Locke), hermeneutics (Dilthey, Gadamer, Betti, Ricoeur), phenomenology (Hegel, Heidegger, Husserl, Merleau-Ponty), existentialism (Nietzsche, Jaspers), critical theory (Horkheimer, Adorno, Habermas), anthropology (Geertz, Turner), symbolic interactionist and critical sociology (Durkheim, Goffman), and humanistic psychology (Freud, Fromm, Mitscherlich). Although such trends in administrative theory became groundwork for a more humanistic approach to public administration in the nineteenth century by political and social theorists, it has not been treated with sufficient depth or acknowledgment. (Haque 1996)

The dominance of new managerialism, in the contemporary and post-NPM sense, driven largely by neo-liberalism, has laid the ground for norms of utility, effectiveness, technology-driven public service, corporate culture, and performances, which override norms previously encased in ethical and socio-cultural theories. Micklethwait and Wooldridge identify four major problems with current managerial trends: "It is constitutionally incapable of self-criticism; that its terminology usually confuses rather than educates; that it rarely rises above basic common sense; and that it is faddish and bedeviled by contradictions that would not be allowed in more rigorous disciplines." (1996, 15)

However, by focusing primarily on the humanistic aspect of the new managerialism approach, it is possible to outline this shift towards a humanistic public administration as a normative one that requires understanding the place of the public servant in the administrative scheme of things. To this we would add the way members of the public service collectively relate to one another within the organizational setting and how this would affect their conception of good public service and, consequently, the formation of a good society. This theoretical foundation is essentially a task of creating a new and timelier meaning to public administration, through which it would become a true service to the benefit of the public; a facilitator rather than a liability. This would be made possible using interpretive and critical methods of learning within the public administration. To that end, the aim of the humanist approach is to entrench a sense of self-understanding oriented towards a unification of the moral and spiritual dimensions of one's work. This is not saying that a humanistic approach leads to better managerial principles of efficiency and effectiveness, but rather one oriented to integrating all human and managerial aspects and capacities of the public servant that directly affect administrative practices.

This chapter aims to articulate Gadamer's work in relation to understanding and interpreting public administration ethics. Hans-Georg Gadamer (1900–2002) was an influential German philosopher in the development of twentieth-century hermeneutics. Gadamer's work inspired an array of disciplines ranging from aesthetics to theology. Hermeneutics is rooted in the Greek word *hermeneutikos* meaning to *interpret*. (Palmer 1969) Hermeneutics engages with the process of human understanding by tracing the meaning of *language* to discover the unlimited possibilities of human thought. (Palmer 1969) For example, the theological interpretations and meaning of the Christian Bible hermeneutics lead to justifying God's authority over human thinking and understanding processes. In contrast, Gadamer's hermeneutics places the ground for empowering human capacity for understanding as a mechanism for effective communication.

Philosophical hermeneutics, according to Gadamer, refers to the concept of understanding. Unlike methodological hermeneutics, philosophical hermeneutics aims "not to ask how understanding occurs in the human sciences, but to ask the question of understanding relative to the entire human experience of the world and the practice of life". (Risser 1997, 9) Gadamer's key concepts are of particular concern for public management using philosophical hermeneutics for building ethics management based on sensory strategies.

Gadamer's theory suggests that understanding *is* interpreting and vice versa, while language acts as the medium. According to Gadamer, understanding in this sense takes place in every aspect of our experiences and is deeply intertwined in all human experience. In essence, he calls on the individual to situate him/herself in the place of the other, by acknowledging the otherness of the other. (Gadamer 2006 [1975]) Thus, philosophical hermeneutics is described as the voice of the other, while being aware of one's own bias.

Gadamerian Philosophical Hermeneutics

Gadamer's concept of understanding is drawn from Logos, a tool to create communication with others. This extends beyond simply thinking and speaking as we "make what is not present manifest through . . . communicat(ing)". (Gadamer 2004, 60–1) For instance, when we think of a certain object, our mind builds a mental image that unconsciously connects our internalized thoughts with the shared and externalized medium of communicating with others. (Gadamer 2004) For that, the process of communicating oneself to another is always linguistically mediated. Such human capacity to convey our thoughts to others is enabled through language. Indeed, Gadamer regards language not as an instrument allowing humans to engage with the world, but rather as the medium for such engagement. It may be suggested that the commonality function of language leads Gadamer's linguisticality of understanding to be captivated within the limitation of our prejudices so that we become biased in our understanding. However, Gadamer views the commonality of language as an essential means for dialogue or conversation. (Gadamer 2004) Gadamer's dialogical approach to hermeneutics calls on the individual to become aware of the constant of preconceptions, whilst being simultaneously open to other ideas that "emerge side by side" until the meaning becomes comprehensible. (Gadamer 2006 [1975], 269) The process of understanding, when it derives from the openness of the hermeneutic process, allows overcoming the limitation of bias.

Three inter-relational aspects relating to language and understanding support Gadamer's claim for the universality of the hermeneutic experience: the *universality* of language, the *forgetfulness* of language, and *I-lessness*. The *universality* of language means that understanding derives from accepting the inner world of subjectivity so that it is through dialogue that language may fill any gaps towards a shared understanding. (Gadamer 2004, 68) The *forgetfulness* of language results from losing the meaning of *what* exists prior to language so that the real being of language begins when we hear what is said. (Gadamer 2004, 64) Finally, *I-lessness*, as the third aspect of language, is understood as participatory. This means that the act of speaking allows us to communicate with others but at the same time to communicate with our inner selves. (Gadamer 2004, 65)

Understanding as Practical Ethics

The three inter-relational aspects of associating language and understanding imply that all understanding has a practical orientation in the sense of being able to apply meaning to our current experience. The applicative or practical form of understanding appears to be linked to Aristotle's notion of Practical Wisdom (*phronesis*). Aristotle's practical wisdom as seen in the previous chapter is a kind of wisdom that for Gadamer demands an understanding of one's situation and context that can be realized only in virtuous living. It is suggested that ethical life is rooted in the capacity to abstract oneself from its own concrete life or acts in favor of the internalization of others' subjective experiences, while staying aware of one's own biases. Viewed in this way, the ethical life derives from a constant dialogical relationship in which we critically examine our own ethical understandings while constantly urging others to do the same.

In this way, Gadamer's ethics, like hermeneutics, begins in life. Gadamer frames daily practices, human life, as intertwined with language. Such association considers our lives as learners. For that, life allows openness to learn by the use of language, especially when we need to articulate our understandings in words, or try to share our understandings, or try to reflect on our understandings. Life is regarded as a space of meaning in which we live and function (traditions, theories, religious beliefs, world pictures, disciplines, communications, ethnicities, identities). Engaging in this space of meaning raises our awareness of others' perspectives and framings. However, being locked up in our regions of meaning does not imply that we are forced to remain within this space. According to Gadamer, our assumptions are taken for granted until "other" competing assumptions cause us to question our current understandings. Gadamer regards this as the process of entering into proper hermeneutic consciousness, which leads to effective self-questioning, which results in the thought "Could it be that I am wrong and they are right?" For Gadamer, this to-and-from interchange of thoughts results in what he defines as "hermeneutic conversation", which allows us to reveal our understanding as partiality and acknowledge the limits of our current understandings. By opening ourselves in a conversation with "the other", we are able to find ourselves changed in certain ways.

What follows from this productive nature of understanding in terms of ethics? Primarily the understanding that the role of rules and principles remains subsidiary. The fact that hermeneutical life is conceived as an ongoing, never-ending process of engagement with the world as a part of it, leads to the notion that we can never come to a complete knowledge of what ethics demands. This is what sets apart ethical knowledge from technical knowledge—the infinite moral engagement driven by an unlimited range of application. Gadamer suggests that an "experienced person" (2006 [1975], 355) is one who does not necessarily have knowledge of everything, nor someone who is cynically never shocked by anything, but rather is someone who is open to transformative encounters with "the other", someone who shares his experience and therefore raises new ways of seeing the world. This, while remaining open to exploring commonalities between their own horizons and those of others involved in hermeneutic conversations. For Gadamer, applicative knowledge derives from learning to be open:

> Experience stands in an ineluctable opposition to knowledge and to the kind of instruction that follows from general theoretical or technical knowledge. The truth of experience always implies an orientation

to new experiences. That is why a person who is called experienced has become so not only *through* experience but is also open *to* new experiences . . . [The experienced person is] someone who is radically undogmatic; who, because of the many experiences he has had and the knowledge he has drawn from them, is particularly well equipped to have new experiences and to learn from them.

(2006 [1975], 355)

By encountering a different horizon of meaning, we become aware of the limits of our existing assumptions in a way that is akin to trial-and-error movement from prejudice to prejudice. (Gadamer 2006 [1975], 353) This engagement with different horizons of meaning is critical in terms of ethical decision-making because genuine hermeneutic experience is inherently a process of awareness of adversities, inadequacies, and illusions of existing understanding: "'Experience' in the genuine sense is always negative. If a new experience of an object occurs to us, this means that hitherto we have not seen the thing correctly and now know it better." (Gadamer 2006 [1975], 353) According to Gadamer, each experience teaches us something new and changes forever our ways. So is the case with ethical decision-making; once an ethical process is underway, it changes forever the way we think, understand, and evaluate similar scenarios in the future. To Gadamer, ethics concerns the ethical and moral imperative to understand others and find commonality (*sensus communis*) in terms of shared understandings rather than shared agreement.

Moreover, it is suggested that we do not choose when and whether to apply ethical knowledge: if we possess this ethical consciousness, it becomes reflected in all of our behaviors and acts. At this point Gadamer insists that, unlike a set of procedural rules or principles, "We do not learn moral knowledge, nor can we forget it." (2006 [1975], 320)

Consequently, public service ethics should be engaged in forging and finding common ground with public management and public administration discipline, and finding a joint application or policy making grounded in practical wisdom (*phronesis*). This emphasis on practical wisdom revitalizes the notion of *Bildung* (Gadamer 2006 [1975], 9–18), which denotes education as a formative action that enables people to become open to being situated "in between" by listening to other perspectives that bring self-reflection. (Wahlström 2010) As articulated by Gadamer:

> *Bildung* requires and enables one to see things through the eyes of others. Wherever it holds sway, it prevents the particular kinds of one-sidedness that goes with school practice, the knowledge gained at college, the mere talent of copying, the pure training of memory.
>
> (Gadamer 2006 [1975], 121)

Such ethics-based practical application is understood as offering practitioners the possibility for personal and professional development as captured by the meaning of *Bildung*. This requires "the skill of being critically distant while remaining involved, attentive, and caring towards the other". (Davey 2006, xvi) It is through this process that one gradually contributes to the other and is being contributed to by the prism of the other, creating a common understanding that serves as the basis for common growth. The process each individual is going through can be referred to as *Bildung*, a key concept in philosophical hermeneutics. (Gadamer 2006 [1975]) *Bildung* mainly represents one's "formation, cultivation and education" (Davey 2006, 37), which can be achieved through interaction with one's cultural, social, and geographical environment. (Kontje 1993) For Gadamer, *Bildung* is the individual's disposition that pursues an inner process of forming and cultivating the self as an intellectual and moral endeavor, while keeping oneself open to the other without sacrificing one's own past, biases, and particularities. Therefore, *Bildung* as a guiding pedagogical approach to form practical ethics cannot be achieved by any merely technical or theoretical means, it must be cultivated out of "an inner process of formation and cultivation, and therefore constantly remains in a state of continual *Bildung*". (Gadamer 2006 [1975], 10)

Gadamer outlines three stages in the application of *Bildung* including:

(1) Unreflected unity with one's natural state and a corresponding disregard of otherness;
(2) Distancing one's natural state induced by otherness;
(3) Understanding between self and other.

Following these stages, *Bildung* always rests on one's own initial viewpoint:

> [If] we overcome the presuppositions [*vorurteile*] and limitations of our previous experience of the world, this does not mean that we leave and negate our own world. Like travelers we return home with new experiences. Even if we emigrate and never return, we still can never wholly forget.
>
> (Gadamer 2006 [1975], 448)

Bildung then requires "transposing oneself" [*sich versetzen*] to broaden each individual's horizon while upholding differences: "For what do we mean by 'transposing ourselves'? Certainly not disregarding ourselves. This is necessary, of course, insofar as we must imagine the other's situation. But into this other situation we must bring, precisely, ourselves." (Gadamer 2006 [1975], 305)

Thus, Gadamer insists that *Bildung* means critically questioning our perspectives more than adopting the standpoints of *others* in order to reach a better understanding of the subject matter: "If we put ourselves in someone else's shoes, for example, then we will understand him—that is, become aware of the otherness, the indissoluble individuality [*individualität*] of the other person—by putting *ourselves* in his position." (Gadamer 2006 [1975], 305)

This last point is crucial for public administrators dealing with matters of ethical significance. Gadamer's notion of *Bildung* enables a stance or gesture of openness to others that requires the public servant to engage their practical wisdom; therefore, an authentic ethics education and management requires the development of a **felt-sense wisdom** enhanced by sensory-based strategies. Gadamer himself outlines the connection between *Bildung* and sense-making, as a "special source of truth". (Gadamer 2006 [1975], 10)

> To recognize one's own in the alien, to become at home in it, is the basic movement of spirit, whose being consists only in returning to itself from what is other . . . every single individual who raises himself out of his natural being to the spiritual finds in the language, customs, and institutions of his people a pre-given body of material, which as in learning to speak, he has to make his own . . . that is what, following Hegel, we emphasized as the general characteristic of Bildung: keeping oneself open to what is other.
>
> (Gadamer 2006 [1975], 13, 15)

Gadamer's notion of *Bildung* thus resonates tantalizingly with the idea of felt-sense so that public servants need the "sense", bodily depth, and groundedness as a way of knowing with and through the senses (Gendlin 1997 [1962], 1–5) to allow a clear space for listening and for unbiased dialogue. But how can the senses be drawn on hermeneutically to make sense and enable *Bildung* or understanding in the public service? It is suggested that metaphors arising from sensory experience may function as a mechanism for generating new understanding and, in turn, can progressively revise the pre-understanding/prejudice as referred to by Gadamer. When tasked with managing complex ethical matters, the public servant has to engage in a dialogic process to develop new understanding and meaning from others' perspectives. That is to say, he or she is expected to follow the codified ethical standard while fitting public service practice to the uniqueness of the other's circumstances without neglecting his or her own perspective. (Brady and Hart 2006) Our aim in the subsequent chapters is to develop the way the sensory experience serves as a rich source of metaphors for generating *Bildung* and facilitating ethics management in the public service.

Bibliography

Brady, F. Neil, and David W. Hart. 2006. "An Aesthetic Theory of Conflict in Administrative Ethics." *Administration & Society* 38.1:113–34.

Davey, Nicholas. 2006. *Unquiet Understanding: Gadamer's Philosophical Hermeneutics*. Albany: State University of New York Press.

Gadamer, Hans-Georg. 2006 [1975]. *Truth and Method*, 2nd ed. New York: Continuum.

———. 2004. *Philosophical Hermeneutics*, 2nd ed. Translated and edited by David E. Linge. Berkeley: University of California Press.

Gendlin, Eugene T. 1997 [1962]. *Experiencing and the Creation of Meaning*. Evanston, IL: Northwestern University Press.

Haque, M. Shamsul. 1996. "The Intellectual Crisis in Public Administration in the Current Epoch of Privatization." *Administration & Society* 27.4:510–36.

Kontje, Todd Curtis. 1993. *The German Bildungsroman: History of a National Genre*. Columbia, SC: Camden House.

Micklethwait, John, and Adrian Wooldridge. 1996. *The Witch Doctors: What the Management Gurus Are Saying, Why It Matters and How to Make Sense of It*. London: Heinemann.

Palmer, Richard E. 1969. *Hermeneutics: Interpretation Theory in Schleiermacher, Dilthey, Heidegger and Gadamer*. Evanston, IL: Northwestern University Press.

Risser, James. 1997. *Hermeneutics and the Voice of the Other: Re-Reading Gadamer's Philosophical Hermeneutics*. Albany: State University of New York Press.

Wahlström, Ninni. 2010. "Do We Need to Talk to Each Other? How the Concept of Experience Can Contribute to an Understanding of *Bildung* and Democracy." *Educational Philosophy and Theory* 42.3:293–309.

3   Understanding through Metaphors

This chapter aims to shed light on the role of metaphors in ethics management. The present chapter provides an overview of how metaphors work and enter into the composition of the political science discipline in general and public administration in particular. We then explore the implications for public administration ethics on claims that metaphors can facilitate new ways of understanding.

The way we think, the way we make sense of the world around us, is mediated through metaphors. As articulated by Mangham (1996, 20):

> Metaphor is an aspect of our lives so ordinary that we use it every day automatically and unconsciously and with so little effort that we rarely find occasion to remark upon it. Whatever our pedigree or education, our waking thoughts and probably our sleeping ones are shaped by metaphor. It is not—most decidedly not—merely a matter of words.

Metaphors function as more than a poetic device, they have been used by humans since earlier times to form thought and action. (Lakoff and Johnson 1999) Snodgrass and Coyne (1991) outline the Greek origins of the word metaphor (*metaphora*), meaning transfer. According to Lakoff and Johnson (1980, 3): "Metaphor is pervasive in everyday life, not just in language but in thought and action. Our ordinary conceptual system, in terms of which we both think and act, is fundamentally metaphorical in nature." Metaphors can be used positively and negatively. They have the power to generate new meanings and improve understanding; however, they can be used to manipulate and to reinforce social powers and ideologies and therefore to hamper thinking. As such, a comprehensive and over-arching conceptualization of metaphor effects is drawn from cognitive psychological studies. (Bodenhausen and Macrae 1998; Chaiken 1980; Entman 2004; Fiske and Kinder 1981; Gilbert and Hixon 1991; Iyengar 1991; Kinder and Sears 1985; Lakoff 1993; Lakoff and Johnson 1980; Ottati and Wyer 1993; Pennington and Hastie 1986; Petty and Cacioppo 1986; Wyer and Srull 1989)

In order to capture the power of metaphors we need to discern the way they operate. Metaphors are assumed to generate an effect by comparing two things that are both similar and dissimilar. (Camp 2005) The components of a metaphor are namely a vehicle and a tenor. The vehicle is a concept that we are familiar with and for that, represents the tenor, while the tenor is the concept being represented in a metaphor. Using a metaphor entails at first the *tertium comparationis*, that is, the common ground between the two concepts that allows additional information about the vehicle. The tenor is not really important in itself, it only "transfers" the information about the vehicle. To identify the common ground, one should realize the way metaphor constructs a link between otherwise distinct conceptual domains. In creating connection across conceptual domains, similarities between the familiar and the unfamiliar concepts can be made by comparing both concepts based on external features (visual), common functions (functional), or organizational structures of both the familiar and unfamiliar concepts. In any case, any structural similarities can be applied in order to transfer our knowledge about the vehicle to the tenor and thus to make sense of the unfamiliar concept. That being said, metaphors help us to gain better understanding of something that might otherwise be too complex or too abstract for our mind to grasp. Conceptual metaphors make abstract concepts more concrete and therefore bring them within our reach.

In their book *Metaphors We Live By*, Lakoff and Johnson state that metaphors can create or lead to new understandings since they are capable of transforming one concept to another: "The essence of metaphor is understanding and experiencing one kind of thing in terms of another." (1980, 5) But how do metaphors structure our understanding? Johnson (Lakoff and Johnson 1999) illustrates this by reconstructing the phrase: "I see what you're saying". He reconstructs the sentence to its metaphorical source domain; that is, seeing while knowing the subject matter. Thus, seeing becomes correlated with knowing. Such correlation arises out of the embodied functioning in the world, where we regularly face cases in which seeing correlates with knowledge. Thus, the source domain of the metaphor emerges from the body's sensorimotor system.

Engagement with metaphors has the potential to invoke the active process of meaning; that is, to bring new understandings into a relationship with the receiver (listener) to learn more of the unfamiliar concept. (Schön 1979) Viewed in this way, metaphors have an important role in the early stages of theoretical development. Weick (1989) defines the role of metaphors in theory development as "disciplined imagination". This notion implies that the process is that in which researchers themselves actively construct representations—representations that outline the field's competing philosophical and scientific foundations and models—to organize knowledge as "theorists are both the source of variation and the source of selection". (Weick 1989, 520) The concept "disciplined imagination" denotes how metaphor can function as the vehicle through which imagination creates tenor and as the source—as a simulated image—for theoretical representations of phenomena that are often complex and abstract. (Cornelissen 2002) Such a methodological contribution of metaphors is illustrated by Weick (1989, 529): "Theorists depend on pictures, maps, and metaphors to grasp the object of study", and "have no choice [in this], but can be more deliberate in the formation of these images and more respectful of representations and efforts to improve them".

Schön (1993) advocates Weick's conceptualization of metaphors by referring to the "generative" feature of metaphor. According to Schön, metaphor functions as "a process by which new perspectives on the world come into existence" (1993, 137), thus ascribing to metaphor a heuristic role for its capacity to enable new understandings to emerge. (Lakoff 1993, 244; Tsoukas 1991; Weick 1989) From this point of view, metaphors enable theorists and researchers to exhibit a coherent body of knowledge and understandings for complex and abstract phenomena that "allows us to refer to it, quantify it, identify a particular aspect of it . . . and perhaps even believe that we understand it" (Lakoff and Johnson 1980, 26). Metaphors are also capable of being involved in relations with a wide array of other ideas or concepts and thereby opening up new and multiple meanings. This process is defined as unlimited and never-ending: "Metaphors and models do not have static, one-off meanings, but are potentially capable of revealing multiple meanings, which can be progressively disclosed by the to-and-fro movement of the hermeneutic circle." (Snodgrass and Coyne 1991, 15) In addition, sensory-based metaphors that are closely connected to bodily experience allow conventional mental imagery that facilitates understanding. (Sopory and Dillard 2002)

To conclude, the discourse on how metaphors work offers important insights on different contemporary theories of the role of metaphors.

Metaphors as Stirring Emotions

The theory that metaphors are evocative suggests that metaphors are used to produce emotional responses to situations. In Way's evocative model of metaphor, metaphors are defined as a rhetorical device by conveying an emotional response to communicate a particular phenomenal state, relating to a particular experience. A metaphor thus become "meaningless, and it is only the emotive effect that a metaphor can produce . . . [and they are] insightful only to the extent they stimulate the emotions of the hearer". (Way 1994, 31) Underlying this account, with its emphasis on positivist views of metaphor, metaphor "works" by creating unexpected reaction. As explained by Henle: "The outstanding characteristic of metaphor is the sort of shock which it produces." (Henle 1958, quoted in Mooij 1976, 18) Such effect involves "new ways of seeing" and thus encourages making more salient (and enriching) phenomenal state attitudes. (Schön 1979) Let us consider the following example: "My love is like a red, red rose." By appealing to the metaphor of the "rose" with its sensory experience, e.g., the way it looks and smells, the feeling evoked by "my love" leads to a focus on how the experience of someone's love might be a similar kind of experience. Other use of metaphors to create certain effects is by "hiding of truth in figures" as stated by Coyne (1995, 261–2). Coyne refers to the capacity of metaphors to produce irrational connections in advancing information technology design, e.g., the use of the concept "windows" for a computer operating system. (Coyne 1995)

Petty and Cacioppo (1986) describe the way metaphors combine the rational with the irrational to stir emotion by referring to the structure of persuasion. A persuasive message is mediated through the central (logical) versus the peripheral (emotional) route of persuasion. While the central route involves the standard information-processing model of decision-making, the peripheral involves the emotional aspect of decision-making resulting from a person's association with positive or negative cues in the stimulus. (Petty and Cacioppo 1986) For example, political metaphors as a persuasive device for political leaders or candidates to legitimize their worldview enable stirring emotions by combining the rational with the irrational to share perception of what is right or wrong:

> Persuasiveness of a non-rational kind persists in natural language particularly in the ethical use of words. Ethical language, words used to convey concepts relates to value judgment, of duty, moral obligations, of feelings towards things, people and events (like "duty" and "ought", "good", "bad", "right", and "wrong") appear not to carry information in terms of knowledge or beliefs but to convey manner or to exhort.
>
> (Jamieson 1985, 74)

Metaphors as Comparisons

A comparison theory of how metaphor works draws on the similarity that exists between two concepts conjoined on a metaphor explicitly or implicitly: "A metaphor compares things without spelling out the comparison." (Bateson 1972, 56) Fogelin suggests that the focus in metaphor is comparison of domains to determine the type of relations between the two concepts embedded in a metaphor:

> To put it soberly . . . Lakoff and Johnson have not shown, as they claim, that most of our normal conceptual system is metaphorically structured . . . but instead, that most of our normal conceptual system is structured through comparison. With this rephrasing, a seeming paradox is replaced by a claim that probably no-one will deny, even if it hasn't been taken seriously enough.
>
> (Fogelin 1988, 86)

Despite Fogelin's criticism, Lakoff and Johnson (1980, 153) do consider a comparison account of metaphor: "X is like Y, in respects A, B, C", and they conclude that "Metaphors *can be* based on isolated similarities" (emphasis added). However, for Lakoff and Johnson, comparison theory cannot account for the fact that metaphors produce inferences beyond the similarities required for their comparison.

Schön (1979, 260) criticizes the comparison theory for ignoring other features of metaphors, namely the fact that they are emergent. Such a mechanism is neglected when viewing metaphors as comparisons and therefore can be "seriously misleading". Once the metaphor has been invoked, new meanings and understandings can be raised and move on to *create* similarities. (Hausman 1989; Lakoff and Johnson 1980; Way 1994) The second challenge to comparison theory lies in the fact that comparison is inherently selective, and that only some of the many features of either concept can be regarded as similar. (see Searle 1983 [1969]; Way 1994, 38) Fogelin emphasizes the choice involved in comparison that reduces some of the features for the sake of similarity statements that "depends upon canons of similarity determined by the context". (Fogelin 1988, 91) A third challenge to comparison theory deals with reinforcing dissimilarities rather than similarities. (Hausman 1989) Comparison theory relies on shared features, while dissimilarities are more profound in generating new understandings than a rendering of pre-existing similarities between the conjoined concepts. (Oswick, Keenoy, and Grant 2002)

Metaphors as Substitutions

The substitution theory suggests that metaphors can be replaced by equivalent literal expression. By drawing on Eco's linguistic and semiotic essays, "metaphors are used to: i) '[substitute]' one expression for another in order to produce an expansion (or a 'condensation') of knowledge at the semantic level" (Eco 1990, 139); and ii) enhance rhetoric: "The status of metaphor . . . is that of mere ornamentation: an author chooses to use it instead of a literal equivalent for reasons of style and decoration." (Way 1994, 34) The fact that metaphorical statement might be replaced by an equivalent literal comparison leads to considering the comparison theory as a special case of a substitution theory. Criticism of the substitution theory of invoking a comparison to paraphrase metaphors indicates that "If familiar literal expressions can be substituted for metaphors, then metaphors will reduce to what was antecedently known." (Hausman 1989, 28)

Metaphors as Interactions

The interaction theory pioneered by Max Black (1962, 1993 [1979]) suggests that metaphors "work" in terms of an interaction, or tension, between two given entities whose attributes are defined prior to the established relation between them: "When we use a metaphor we have two thoughts of different things active together and supported by a single word or phrase, whose meaning is a resultant of their interaction." (Black 1962, 38; see also Cornelissen 2002; Gibbs 1992; Katz 1992; Shannon 1992; Shen 1997; Tourangeau and Sternberg 1982)

Black uses the following metaphor: "John is a wolf". (1962, 28) The first part of the sentence "John is" is the frame of the metaphor while the second part "a wolf" is the focus of the metaphor. Black's interaction approach of metaphor means that the focus of the metaphor must attain a new meaning through the conjunction of the frame and the focus. The new meaning, as articulated by Black "is not quite its meaning in literal uses, nor quite the meaning which any literal substitute would have". (Black 1962, 39) The new meaning is established through "associated commonplaces". (Black 1962, 40) The associated commonplaces incorporate all those ideas one associates with John (e.g., works at a bank, married to Judy, prefers his scotch with soda) and all of the ideas one associates with wolves (move in a pack, eat small animals, communicate through barking). (Ayoob 2007)

The commonplaces associated with both the frame and the focus, e.g., covered in fur, (hairy) wolf creates a new meaning for the focus (the wolf). As Black explains:

> Suppose I look at the night sky through a piece of heavily smoked glass on which certain lines have been left clear. Then I shall see only the stars that can be made to lie on the lines previously prepared upon the screen, and the stars I do see will be seen as organized by the screen's structure. We can think of a metaphor as such a screen and the system of "associated commonplaces" of the focal word as the network of lines upon the screen. We can say that the principle subject is "seen through" the metaphorical expression, or, if we prefer, that the principal subject is "projected upon" the field of the subsidiary subject.
>
> (Black 1962, 41)

These two groups of commonplaces are reduced to only those that may be shared by both: the process through which the focus of the metaphor overlooks unwanted commonplaces of both groups results in a change that fosters new understanding. Yet Black's system of associated commonplaces neglects to explain why the focus of the metaphor is in some way more primary or accessible and able to affect the commonplaces of the frame. The root source of such criticism tends to obscure the failure of Black's theory to explain how the focus is actually distinguished from frame.

Locating metaphors in interaction theory is also central in Ricoeur's (1978 [1975]) and later in Coyne's (1995) studies. Rather than selecting a particular set of associated commonplaces, metaphors work through the tension between sameness and difference. The ability to work toward sameness in spite of the overwhelming presence of difference, allows new meanings to emerge with a metaphor. (Coyne 1995, 296) It should be noted that this theory of interaction corresponds with Hans-Georg Gadamer's theory of hermeneutics that interpretation of the parts of the metaphor within a given context gives a way of appreciating and creating diverse understandings.

Stone (1988) suggests that metaphor interaction and comparison approaches can amalgamate by activating a story line or narrative. This connection can be activated since:

> Metaphors are important devices for strategic representation in political analysis. On the surface, they simply draw a comparison between one thing and another, but in a more subtle way, they usually imply a whole narrative story and a perception for action.
>
> (Stone 1988, 118)

The narrative story line can be conceptualized as an event representation or script that guides understanding, interpretation, and opinion formation that are based on communication. (Berinsky and Kinder 2006; Pennington and Hastie 1986)

In sum, all these theories refer to how metaphors work and the potential for changed understandings to emerge. The diversity of views on metaphor and how it works is mirrored by the variety of aspects including whether the meanings of metaphors relate to speaker/author intentions; whether metaphors are based on similarities or dissimilarities; whether the meanings of metaphors can be literally paraphrased; whether metaphors have no meaning beyond their respective literal meanings; and whether metaphors are a mechanism for understanding. (Bontekoe 1987; Eco 1983; Gibbs 1992; Lakoff and Johnson 1980; Searle 1983) Gibbs (1992) has demonstrated that the differences between theories of metaphor lie in their temporal stages in the process of understanding metaphorical expressions. Underlying Gibbs' view, "Theories of metaphor do not necessarily compete with one another, but can be evaluated through an appreciation of the specific time-course that underlies metaphor understanding." (1992, 575)

Approaching metaphors through the process of understanding allows us to view their role as creating or leading to new understandings. (Snodgrass and Coyne 1991) The account we therefore develop and elaborate in this book involves the use of metaphors to communicate existing knowledge and professional practice in bringing understanding through interaction metaphors. As such, metaphors

> play a decisive role in the (re)ordering of knowledge and thus serve as prime targets and tools of analyses in the realm of knowledge dynamics. Their transferability and their linkage function, in particular, allow study of the (at times) inconspicuous mechanisms of knowledge production.
>
> (Maasen and Weingart 2000, 37)

It is this point above all else that has implications for ethical reasoning and practice in the public service. In what follows, we discuss the way metaphors operate across disciplinary fields such as organizational studies, political science, and public administration.

The Application of Metaphors in Organizational Studies

Viewing metaphors as a heuristic device within the organizational field has gained prominence in both academics' and practitioners' discourses. (Barley and Kunda 1992; Cornelissen 2002; Driver 2002; Easterby-Smith 1997; Morgan 1980, 1983, 2006; Oswick, Keenoy, and Grant 2002; Pinder and Bourgeois 1982; Putnam and Boys 2006; Tsoukas 1991) Morgan (2011) suggested that metaphors have profound implications for developing strategies to shape perceptions in organizations. The emergence and appeal of metaphors in organizational studies underlies the idea that metaphors help to communicate new and/or existing knowledge:

> Metaphors provide partial insights; that different metaphors can produce conflicting insights; that in elevating one insight others are downplayed; that a way of seeing becomes a way of not seeing; and that any attempt to understand the complex nature of organizations (as with any complex subject) always requires an open and pluralistic approach based on the interplay of multiple perspectives.
>
> (Morgan 2011, 475)

Research on the role of metaphors in organizational studies has found correspondence across academic disciplines, introducing new perspectives to the knowledge dynamic and understanding within the organizational field:

> It [i.e., metaphor analysis] looks for both the locally specific processings of metaphors and the ways in which they—gradually—produce (heterogeneous sets of) meanings across (various types of) discourses for a given period of time. Admittedly, the goal of metaphor analysis is not a modest one. It attempts to surface nothing less than the anatomy of the grand phenomena in the changing world of knowledge, be it paradigm shifts, the emergence of a new Zeitgeist, or the rise and fall of general worldviews.
>
> (Maasen and Weingart 2000, 4)

Approaching metaphor in this interdisciplinary manner underlies the idea that metaphorical analysis is a valuable device for liberation and widening the scope of organization and management theory. (Morgan 2006) Popular metaphors used in organizational studies and carried by practitioners as well, at least in part, are corporate culture, organizational identity, and organizational learning.

The learning organization metaphor, for example, addressed the problem of how learning and cognition at the collective and organizational levels occur in the postmodern era, where organizations form "learning sites". (e.g., Easterby-Smith 1997; Fiol and Lyles 1985; Schneider and Angelmar 1993; Walsh 1995) Scholarly theorizing through organizational learning established horizons of meanings as it developed along with other metaphors of organizational cognition and learning such as "organizational mind" (Sandelands and Stablein 1987) and "organizational memory". (Walsh 1995; Walsh and Ungson 1991) The metaphor of learning organization is based on similarity between two entities: organization and learning. The mental, cognitive act of learning occurs at the individual and organizational levels, implying the need for a unified agency that is capable of learning. As a result of ascribing the concept of agency to the learning process made by a collective whole, the learning organization metaphor signified a paradigmatic return to traditional functionalist and holistic models. From the functionalist perspective, learning is not conceived in terms of aggregation of the cognition of its individual members but rather with how individuals learn in a way that is conducive to the organization's aims and needs. (Argyris 1999; DiBella, Nevis, and Gould 1996; Hendry 1996; Jankowicz 2000; Jones 1990; Simon 1991; see also Argryis and Schön 1978) While the functionalist account of organizational learning metaphor did not embrace all types of learning processes conducted in organizations, it facilitated managerial strategies on improving employees' commitment to shared values and corporate objectives through organizational artifacts, e.g., codes of conduct, codes of ethics. (Antonacopoulou 1998, 2001; Crossan, Lane, and White 1999; Kim 1993; Nonaka 1994; Nonaka and Takeuchi 1995; Walsh and Ungson 1991)

The Application of Metaphors in Political Studies

The role of metaphors in political inquiry has been assumed to extend political knowledge or to reinforce aspects that previously were considered not salient. (Howe 1988; Landau, Meier, and Keefer 2010; Landau, Sullivan, and Greenberg 2009; Miller 1979; Mio 1996, 1997) As Landau contended: "Political science has always resorted to metaphors, to the device of proceeding from the known to the unknown. Those who criticize the use of models need to understand that they too must use them." (1972, 101–2) Politicians use metaphors in their speeches, suggesting that metaphors can enthuse the electorate, influence public opinion, or raise awareness toward a certain political matter. (Mio et al. 2005) Beer and de Landtsheer (2004, 24) indicate that politicians use metaphors "as tools of persuasive communication, to bridge gaps and build identification between strangers; to frame issues; to create, maintain, or dissolve political coalitions; to generate votes and win elections." Metaphors are prevalent in many forms of the political field such as metaphors involving family, e.g., "players" on the president's "team"; "Rainbow coalition" (Howe 1988); metaphors in policy decision-making, e.g., "cutting fat" from a budget; metaphors in international relations and strategy involving war, conflict, and terrorism e.g., "cold war", "brainwashing", "detente"; metaphors in social policy and immigration, e.g., "melting pot", "war on poverty"; metaphors involving nature, e.g., "grassroots", "heads of state"; metaphors in political communication, e.g., spin; and metaphors in ethics, e.g., whistleblower, and so on. (Eubanks 2000; Gilbert 1979; Howe 1988; Kruglanski et al. 2007; O'Brien 2003; Ottati, Rhoads, and Graesser 1999)

Studies in political research discuss how metaphors operate from a variety of different perspectives. In Aristotle's earliest writings, metaphor interpretation involved a comparison of objects by discerning certain reciprocity or relations to explicate the similarity that exists between the two objects. (Aristotle 1991) In *The Rhetoric* (1410b), Aristotle addresses the instructive value of metaphor:

> To learn easily is naturally pleasant to all people, and words signify something, so whatever words create knowledge in us are the pleasantest . . . Metaphor most brings about learning; for when [Homer] calls old age "stubble," he creates understanding and knowledge through the genus, since both old age and stubble are [species of the genus of] things that have lost their bloom.

Hobbes is more ambivalent about the role of metaphors and their appropriateness in political inquiry while using multiple metaphors including a metaphor in the title of his manuscript: *Leviathan*. (Cantalupo 1988) Hobbes downsizes the role of metaphors on the grounds that they are employed to deceive and mislead others (1996, 36):

(1a) To conclude, The Light of humane minds is Perspicuous Words, but by exact definitions first snuffed, and purged from ambiguity; *Reason* is the *pace*, Encrease of *Science*, the *way*; and the Benefit of man-kind, the *end*.

(1b) And on the contrary, Metaphors, and senslesse and ambiguous words, are like *ignes fatui*;

(1c) and reasoning upon them, is wandering amongst innumerable absurdities; and their end, contention, and sedition, or contempt.

Following Hobbes' line of reasoning on how metaphors operate in political inquiry, there are some concerns with the application of metaphors in the political field. The first problem concerns the capacity of metaphors in making obscure and ambiguous political ideas and concepts clear. As seen, the role of metaphor is defined as a linguistic medium for transmitting meanings from the familiar to the unfamiliar. From this perspective, the role of metaphor is seen as rather methodological as a specific communication strategy with the purpose of capturing the dynamics of the political world. (Landau, Sullivan, and Greenberg 2009) The obscurity and ambiguity of political ideas initially arises from the fact that they cannot be observed directly by the senses. As Miller explains:

> It is simply impossible to perceive the political in the immediate or direct way that we experience bodies and their sensible qualities, including our own bodies. Insofar as political things have an embodiment, that bodily aspect is perceptible, but the shapes and qualities that are given to the senses can always be accounted for as something in themselves, so that there is no necessity to see them as something else, something political. We like to speak of observing political behavior, but all that we can actually perceive with the senses are motions of limbs, facial expressions, articulate sounds, and artifacts of one sort or another. Strictly speaking, therefore, political things are unobservable things.
>
> (Miller 1979, 163)

Metaphor's capacity for transference as drawn from the field of observable and tangible objects is of special importance when dealing with various aspects of the political realm, e.g., the relationships of human beings, of their nature or soul, and of their place in the world around them. (Howe 1988; Lakoff 2004; Mio 1996, 1997)

The pervasiveness of metaphor in the political realm, however, led to the inability to uncover the hidden dimensions of the metaphor. As Locke noted:

> How great a dependence our words have on common sensible ideas; and how those which are made use of to stand for actions and notions quite removed from sense, have their rise from thence, and from obvious sensible ideas are transferred to more abstruse significations, and made to stand for ideas that come not under the cognizance of our senses; v.g. to imagine, apprehend, comprehend, adhere, conceive, instil, disgust, disturbance, tranquillity, &c., are all words taken from the operations of sensible things, and applied to certain modes of thinking. Spirit, in its primary signification, is breath; angel, a messenger: and I doubt not but, if we could trace them to their sources, we should find, in all languages, the names for things that fall not under our senses to have had their first rise from sensible ideas.
>
> (1959, Vol. 2, 5)

Locke then questions the legitimacy of metaphors in the political sphere by exemplifying the complexity in tracing the sources of metaphors. The implication of such perspective is demonstrated by Edelman (1971, 67):

> Metaphor . . . defines the pattern of perception to which people respond. To speak of deterrence and strike capacity is to perceive war as a game; to speak of legalized murder is to perceive war as a slaughter of human beings . . . Each metaphor intensifies selected perceptions and ignores others, thereby helping one to concentrate upon desired consequences

of favored public policies and helping one to ignore their unwanted, unthinkable, or irrelevant premises and aftermaths. Each metaphor can be a subtle way of highlighting what one wants to believe and avoiding what one does not wish to face.

In this perspective, politicians may use metaphor to frame certain ideas or political issues that do not refer to anything directly observable in the purpose of selective information and arguments they wish to promote while obscuring information and arguments they rather ignore. (Lakoff and Johnson 1980) In the same vein, Van Teeffelen summarizes the power of metaphors to underscore particular elements and linkages, and simultaneously to overlook others:

> Since they organize the understanding of cause and effect, symptom and essence, and especially praise and blame, metaphors can be employed to serve political aims or interests. When thus used as ideological devices, they privilege, and when turning into common sense, naturalize particular accounts of reality.
>
> (1994, 384–6)

Since this problem cannot be resolved by producing empirical facts, one can think of the qualities of sensible things, as these are what we discern first with more distinctness and clarity. It should be noted that not only political metaphors that rely on sensible things exclusively lead to greater clarity. Sources of metaphors such as relationships/family may also transfer meaning despite the fact that they incorporate unobservable dimensions. For example, when a metaphor is applied to fatherhood as a way to characterize political relationships, family relations as a source of metaphor prompt more familiarity than political relations. This is also the case when using the concept of a soul when referring to Kallipolis (the city) and types of regime. (Plato's *The Republic*, 368c-9a) In *The Republic*, Plato uses this analogy to suggest that there cannot be social justice (the city) if each of us maintains internal justice (the soul) in himself. Although the "city" is not a sensible object, nonetheless it is more familiar to us than the soul. Socrates defends this transfer by using the analogy to letters when he suggests that, as with matching big to small letters, the city is bigger and easier to observe than the soul. (Plato's *The Republic*, 368c-9a) This analogy underlies Socrates' assumption that our eyes are unable to transfer meaning. Hume also acknowledges that one "cannot compare the soul more properly to anything than to a republic or commonwealth". (1955, 261 also 415–6)

The second weakness refers to how metaphors in the political realm can make unobservable things apparent. Miller (1979) suggests distinguishing between metaphorical naming and metaphorical reasoning. Metaphorical naming aims to identify something as yet hidden or inaccessible by giving it a name. Naming serves to create or lead to new understandings, therefore extending the names of objects in accordance with the progress of our knowledge. Metaphorical reasoning goes beyond naming in its capacity to sort out likeness or similarity between two concepts as they exemplify a common principle. For example, seeing and knowing refer to different activities, e.g., seeing is a sensory activity while knowing is an intellectual activity. Since both activities are based on cognition, we are able to extend the names and meanings from the common activity of seeing to a rational activity. (McInerny 1968) An additional example from medieval philosophy is the lion and fox metaphor employed by Machiavelli. Such a metaphor helps us to understand that rulers can achieve their purposes by being aware of risk situations before it is too late to avoid harm and by standing courageously against foes. In this metaphor, cunning and courage are principles that characterize the behavior of foxes and lions that are also familiar in human actions. Viewed in this way, metaphors operate in political realm by demarcating a common principle between two objects conjoined in a metaphor.

A third issue concerns the ability to test metaphors applied in the political realm. As seen, metaphors in political inquiry are grounded on a discoverable likeness—not only between two objects or concepts but also between observable and unobservable. For that, metaphors are tied to truth conditions or opinion. (Binkley 1974) Metaphors in the political arena, therefore, can be neither verified nor falsified. Miller suggests that in testing the truth of a metaphor, we must discern based on political experience that provides a setting that enables us to capture the thing in its wholeness:

> In testing the truth of a metaphor, we typically begin by articulating it in other terms as an assertion about reality. Adequacy, however, has to do with the irreducible features of a metaphor, those that are lost in a literal restatement. Adequacy cannot be divorced completely from truth, but it is determined mainly by criteria of style and taste, such as liveliness, freshness, or appropriateness.
>
> (Miller 1979, 167)

Consequently, in the course of inquiry, there is really no limit to what a metaphor can manifest. Therefore, once a political context or knowledge of the speaker determines the relevant "meaning" of the metaphor, the additional effects of metaphor remain outside proper theoretical testing. (Davidson 1979 [1978])

An additional concern is associated with the indispensability of political expression and political knowledge. The role metaphor plays in the pursuit of political knowledge builds on meaningful relationships to political reality. Reflecting on the relation between man and politics cannot be done apart from some metaphor. Ricoeur refers to the interpretive function of metaphor without which political expression and political knowledge remain vague:

> It is a composite discourse, therefore, and as such cannot but feel the opposite pull of two rival demands. On the one side, interpretation seeks

the clarity of the concept; on the other, it hopes to preserve the dyna-
mism of meaning that the concept holds and pins down.

(Ricoeur 1977, 303)

Thompson (1996) once asserted that politics without metaphors is like
a "fish without water". As seen, engagement with metaphors in political
inquiry and discourse allows simplification of complex political issues to an
assumed largely ignorant public and it is therefore the reason for the indispensability of metaphors in political knowledge and communication, despite
the fact that metaphor often has a specific political aim it does not underesti-
mate its role in "creat[ing] social reality and guid[ing] social action". (Lakoff
and Johnson 1980, 156) In this regard, Vavrus (2000, 194) rightly points
out that "Far from simply describing the world, metaphors are prescriptive
linguistic devices that guide and shape thinking as well."

The Application of Metaphors in Public Administration and Management

Public service, like politics, builds heavily on the relationship with human
beings and human society. As previously mentioned in the theoretical overview of the role of metaphors and how they operate, public service should
also abound with metaphors. Theories also suggest that abstract concepts
are understood via metaphor mapping the observable and the familiar onto
the abstract and nonobservable; then how abstract concepts such as public
service values are structured in terms of metaphor in this special field of
public service is of great value for both academic and practitioner communities. For example, despite the increasing scholarly attention to public
service values in the field (e.g., Bozeman 2007; Christensen, Goerdel, and
Nicholson-Crotty 2011; Jørgensen 1999; Kernaghan 2003; Menzel 2003;
van der Wal and Huberts 2008; Van Wart 1998), there is no clear consensus
about the specific role that public service values and norms play in the day-
to-day behavior and decision-making of administrators. As explained by
Van Wart (1998, xviii), the challenge for public administrators is "to achieve
a mixture of values in a workable gestalt or whole" that, in turn, requires an
ongoing "dialectic because of legitimate competition of values and inevitable
shifts in priority".

The proliferation of metaphors in the public service in both academic and
professional discourses has come to be seen by many as steering a paradigmatic shift in the public service. (Stout 2009) Public administration theories
are often viewed as a complex set of philosophical tensions that practitioners need to use in their daily practice. For that, public administration
literature is often organized by the metaphor of "tradition" to enable practitioners to distinguish between competing ideas about the role of public servants and the normative commitments when choosing among them. (Stout
2007) Drawing on the metaphor of "tradition", public administration has
developed as an academic discipline through a number of stages in terms of

paradigms.[1] (Stout 2009) Each paradigm was guided by specific ethos and the corresponding role identity of public servants. (Kettl 2000; McSwite 1997; Newland 2003) In this case, it is the ethos and the professional identity of public servants embedded in metaphors that enabled demarcation of the disciplinary boundary between paradigms.

For example, traditional bureaucratic ethos was promoted by the work of the German sociologist Max Weber (1949, 1968) Weber has laid grounds for the traditional public administration. Weber believed that organizations should be managed impersonally by formal structure and rules of conduct. This was called a bureaucracy. Bureaucracy, in Weberian tradition, defined as a non-personal, objective form of organization, was viewed "as the expression of rational and efficient administration". (Breton and Wintrobe 1985, 33) The underlying idea behind bureaucratic organizations was that they efficiently manage the work of large numbers of people. (Denhardt and Denhardt 2000) The emergence of managerialism and the new public management and governance paradigms advocated client-oriented approaches in the public service, enhancing decentralization of authority and becoming more "businesslike" through the importation of management approaches and techniques from the private sector.

The metaphor "red tape and bureaucracy" is generally associated with centralized, hierarchical, rule-ridden, functionally specialized organizations. The metaphor of red tape usually denotes excessive paperwork (Bennett and Johnson 1979); a high degree of formalization and control (Hall 1968); needless rules, procedures, and regulations; inefficiency; unjustifiable wastefulness; and as a consequence—public distrust and frustration. (Bozeman, Reed, and Scott 1992) Herbert Kaufman (1977) suggests that such a negative image of the public service practice can be lessened if the excessive constraints that are largely structural in nature can be avoided "When people rail against red tape, they mean that they are subjected to too many constraints, that many of the constraints seem pointless, and that agencies seem to take forever to act." Kaufman explains that red tape doesn't necessarily stem from bureaucrats' incompetence but rather from the conflicting public duties inherent in serving as a public administrator. A public servant holds direct responsibility for the welfare of the public, responsibility towards a political superior in executing public policies, as well as to his professional association. This view is articulated as an administrative "tragedy of the commons":

> Every restraint and requirement originates in somebody's demand for it. Of course, each person does not will them all; on the contrary, even the most broadly based interest groups are concerned with only a relatively small band of the full spectrum of government activities . . . But there are so many of us, and such a diversity of interests among us, that modest individual demands result in great stacks of official paper and bewildering procedural mazes.

> (Kaufman 1977, 29)

The Bureaucracy metaphor covers the role of the administrator as a Bureaucrat, whose actions are legitimized as long as they follow formal rules and procedures controlled by the separated powers of the constitutional order, through the organizational hierarchy. (March and Simon 1958) This metaphor reinforces the view that citizens were treated as passive recipients of services. (Stout 2009)

"Line and staff" metaphor signifies the persistent debate initiated by Woodrow Wilson's idea of a politics-administration dichotomy. In his seminal 1887 article "The Study of Administration", Wilson introduces the politics-administration dichotomy based on a functional-structural view of government that is divided into two separate spheres of politics and administration.[2] For Wilson, politics dealt with issues of policy decision-making; administration deals with execution of government decisions. He defined public administration as follows: "Public administration is detailed and systematic execution of public law . . . but the general laws . . . are obviously outside of and above administration. The broad plans of governmental action are not administrative; the detailed execution of such plans is administrative." (Wilson 1966, 372) Such dichotomy was implied in the line and staff metaphor that originated in the military. The distinction between line and staff agencies refers to different functions in an organization. While staff members are involved in planning and decision-making, line members are involved in execution and implementation of those plans and policies.[3] Although line and staff management have two separate hierarchies, a line manager may have direct control over staff employees but a staff manager cannot exert such power over the line employees.

The politics-administration dichotomy entrenched in the line and staff metaphor has paved the way to regard the role of public administrator as "a Hero" and as "an Innocent Victim" in defending the administrators' public image. (Terry 1997) Terry uses these metaphors to show how the politics-administration dichotomy was undertaken during the Reagan era. In his study Terry considers the theater metaphor to symbolize how the relation between public administration and elected officials during the Reagan era reached an intensified political rivalry. During the 1980s, Reagan consistently criticized the advance and expense of the federal bureaucracy. (Dallek 1984; Farazmand 1989; Hubbell 1991a; Lane and Wolf 1990; Rosen 1986) To counter Reagan's attack, advocates of public administration reinvigorated a competing image for the public service by drawing on metaphors such as hero and innocent victim. (Bellavita 1991; Hubbell 1990, 1991b; Terry 1997) By drawing on the ancient hero myth and Campbell's idea of "hero's journey" (1968), Bellavita (1991, 155) suggests that:

> The classic hero myth begins with the kingdom in trouble. Crops are not growing. Babies are not being born. Sickness, alienation, and despair are rampant. Life is vanishing from the land. Some people claim that it is the fault of a sinful and despotic king. Others blame the dragon that

roams the countryside destroying everything in its path. The elders meet to decide what to do, but their ideas have been heard before and no longer have any power. Hope is disappearing from the kingdom. Into the slough of despondency comes the hero, the man or woman who takes on the task of bringing new life to a dying land.

Bellavita constructs the role of public administrators as a hero, to suggest their ability to rise (heroically) above difficulties and adversity and even to make a difference. While Bellavita applies the hero metaphor as a descriptor of public administrators' role conception, Hubbell (1990) offers to use the hero metaphor as a normative prescriptive guide for attitudes and behavior of public administrators when faced with competing values, loyalties, and interests. Viewed in this way, the hero metaphor enables professional socialization of public administrators by developing a sense of pride of belonging to a profession, in motivating individuals to regard themselves as professionals.

An additional metaphor that serves to enhance the public image of public administrators and their professional socialization is the public administrator as innocent victim. (Rosen 1983 (cited in Terry 1997), 1986; Terry 1997; Wildavsky 1988) The innocent victim metaphor is brought from social psychology study to raise public sympathy towards public administrators who happen to remain powerless and vulnerable against the unwarranted and irresponsible attacks from politicians. As Rosen puts it (1983, 41–2 (cited in Terry 1997)):

> Government bureaucrats are silent victims of irresponsible criticism . . . too often the isolated shortcomings of government bureaucrats are generalized into McCarthy-type smears on the performance of all employees. Many politicians and business executives engage in this irresponsible rhetoric, and unfortunately print and electronic journalists often carry their unjustified condemnation far and wide . . . many conclude that the unwarranted savaging of government bureaucracies creates intolerable working conditions . . . I believe public employees can reverse this ever worsening trend, and by doing so they will benefit the nation and themselves. They must resolve through their unions, professional societies, and other associations that they will no longer serve as silent and helpless victims in the unjustified broadside leveled at government bureaucracies.

The attractiveness of the innocent victim metaphor was embedded in what Wildavsky (1988) calls "ideological dissensus" for the rivalry between Democratic and Republican parties regarding the role of government. (Terry 1997, 57) According to Wildavsky (1988, 753, 755),

> In a little piece on leadership, Irving Spitzberg, Jr. writes about the "ubiquitous anomie . . . throughout the federal service." That seems to

describe the situation pretty well. Things are bad and are unlikely to get better. Civil servants by themselves cannot do much to improve the situation because their situation is the effect not the cause. He further states: Security of tenure has . . . been weakened. The legal rights of civil servants are now counterbalanced by the rights others have against them. When their units go, so may they . . . Bureaucracy used to means security, now it means exposure.

In the late 1980s, yet another ethos of public administration began to displace the last one. It signifies a deviation from the traditional bureaucratic management of public services towards a more entrepreneurial management, which came to be called the New Public Management (NPM). (Denhardt and Denhardt 2000) The management approach to public service ideas and practices is proposed by David Osborne and Ted Gaebler in their book *Reinventing Government.* (1993) Osborne and Gaebler proposed to shape administrators' professional identity: "To complement the efficiency and effectiveness of market mechanisms, we need the warmth and caring of families and neighborhoods and communities. As entrepreneurial governments move away from administrative bureaucracies, they need to embrace both markets and community." (1993, 309) Since efficiency was considered the main challenge of public administration (Rosenbloom 1983, 220), businesslike methods and the introduction of quality management techniques were conceived as appropriate tools to enhance improved public service delivery and performance. In this vein, Osborne and Plastrik (1997, 130–1) suggest that:

> The most powerful approach is to force public service delivery organizations to function as business enterprises with financial bottom lines, preferably in competitive markets. We call this *enterprise management.* Rather than acquiring their government revenues from government appropriations of tax dollars, these public enterprises earn money by selling goods and services directly to their customers. To earn their keep, in other words, they must succeed in the marketplace.

The paradigm emerging under the NPM is that "entrepreneurial" government envisioned businesslike values and guiding principles to rearrange division of responsibilities within government (Osborne and Gaebler 1993, xviii), as noted by Osborne and Gaebler:

> Most entrepreneurial governments promote *competition* between service providers. They *empower* citizens by pushing control out of the bureaucracy, into the community. They measure the performance of their agencies, focusing not on inputs but on *outcomes.* They are driven by their goals—their *missions*—not by their rules and regulations. They redefine their clients as *customers* and offer them choices . . . They

prevent problems before they emerge, rather than simply offering services afterward. They put their energies into *earning* money, not simply spending it. They *decentralize* authority, embracing participatory management. They prefer *market* mechanisms to bureaucratic mechanisms. And they focus not simply on providing public services, but on *catalyzing* all sectors—public, private, and voluntary—into action to solve their community problems.

(1993, 19–20)

The metaphor of businesslike that accompanied the paradigm shift from public administration to new public management involves a move in cutting the cost of public service provision, while, at the same time, increasing its quality. It allows demarcation of a sharp contrast with the old metaphor of bureaucracy as the organizing structure of public administration and promised an entrepreneurial government based on less centralized structure and institutional mechanism to improve public accountability and effective provision of public services. (deLeon and Denhardt 2000; Maesschalck 2004)

The new public management paradigm also empowers the role of elected officials to possess greater discretionary power and public administrators as discretionary experts who are responsible for desirable policy outputs. The new framing for this role pattern of civil servants is provided by the metaphor of "public administrator as an entrepreneur" that, unlike the traditional metaphor of public administrator as a bureaucrat who follows established rules and regulations and possesses little or no discretion and with no direct responsibility, as an entrepreneur he or she exercises decision-making authority over, and responsibility for, the public service he or she delivers.

The concept of metaphor that underlies studies of this type holds an intriguing promise for understanding the ways in which people construct their realities. One can assume that the speech used by teachers, or by other professionals when they talk about their work, represents something to them. If the speech is metaphorical, then it is reasonable to believe that the metaphors used reflect something of how the speaker sees or constructs professional reality. If the metaphors are used persistently, then the case for their representing a construction of reality becomes more compelling.

Our purpose in this chapter was twofold: (1) to discuss how metaphor operates, and thus a more useful approach towards studying and understanding the ethics management dynamics within the public service field; and (2) to arrive at an enriched understanding and deeper appreciation of the role of metaphor across academics' and practitioners' studies. Reflections on the application of dominant metaphors in the public administration field illustrate that public administration has provided fertile soil for the growth of metaphors. Metaphors serve to increase the accessibility or understanding of certain aspects of professional practice and to improve the profession's reputation, thus developing a deep sense of commitment to professional guiding principles and pride among professional community members. Framed as such, we suggest that to meaningfully reflect upon and act in the public interest, ethical reasoning should involve the use of metaphors.

The ability to meaningfully reflect upon and act in the public interest involves the use of moral reasoning. As Bozeman explains, the public interest is an intangible concept that implies an ideal that in some particular context "refers to the outcomes best serving the long-run survival and well-being of a social collective construed as a public". (2007, 12) It is suggested that metaphors can enhance public administrators' capacity for moral reasoning of the public interest and its engagement with other conflicting public values such as efficiency, effectiveness, justice, respect for individual rights, accountability, and "providing normative consensus about (a) the rights, benefits, and prerogatives to which citizens should (and should not) be entitled; (b) the obligations of citizens to society, the state, and one another; and (c) the principles on which governments and policies should be based." (Bozeman 2007, 13) In what follows, we briefly discuss sensory-based metaphors and their role in improving understanding of public service values and ethical guiding principles.

Notes

1. See Henry's typology of paradigms in the public service (2010, 27): paradigms under the politics-administration dichotomy (1887–1926); principles of public administration (1927–37); public administration as political science (1950–70); public administration as management (1950–70); public administration as public administration (1970–present); and governance (1990–present).
2. It should be noted that Wilson, in his later writings supported a "business-like" government to advance efficiency in the public sector. (Wilson 1966) However, the idea put forth in "The Study of Administration" is that public administration should not be treated or transformed into a private sector.
3. For a detailed conceptualization of the line and staff metaphor, see Taylor (1967).

Bibliography

Antonacopoulou, Elena P. 1998. "Developing Learning Managers within Learning Organisations." In *Organisational Learning and the Learning Organisation: Developments in Theory and Practice*, edited by Mark Easterby-Smith, Luis Araujo, and John Burgoyne, 214–42. London: Sage Publications.

———. 2001. "The Paradoxical Nature of the Relationship between Training and Learning." *Journal of Management Studies* 38.3:327–50.

Argyris, Chris. 1999. *On Organizational Learning*, 2nd ed. Oxford: Blackwell Publishers.

———, and Donald A. Schön. 1978. *Organizational Learning*. Boston, MA: Addison-Wesley.

Aristotle. 1991. *On Rhetoric: A Theory of Civil Discourse*. Translated by George A. Kennedy. New York: Oxford University Press.

Ayoob, Emily. 2007. "Black & Davidson on Metaphor." *Malcalester Journal of Philosophy* 16.1:56–64.

Barley, Stephen R., and Gideon Kunda. 1992. "Design and Devotion: Surges of Rational and Normative Ideologies of Control in Managerial Discourse." *Administrative Science Quarterly* 37:363–99.

Bateson, Gregory. 1972. *Steps to an Ecology of Mind: Collected Essays in Anthropology, Psychiatry, Evolution and Epistemology*. London: Intertext Books.

Beer, Francis A., and Christ'l de Landtsheer, eds. 2004. *Metaphorical World Politics*. East Lansing, MI: Michigan State University Press.

Bellavita, Christopher. 1991. "The Public Administrator as Hero." *Administration & Society* 23:155–85.

Bennett, James T., and Manuel H. Johnson. 1979. "Paperwork and Bureaucracy." *Economic Inquiry* 17:435–51.

Berinsky, Adam J., and Donald R. Kinder. 2006. "Making Sense of Issues through Media Frames: Understanding the Kosovo Crisis." *Journal of Politics* 68:640–56.

Binkley, Timothy. 1974. "On the Truth and Probity of Metaphor." *Journal of Aesthetics and Art Criticism* 33:171–80.

Black, Max. 1962. *Models and Metaphor*. Ithaca: Cornell University Press.

———. 1993 [1979]. "More about Metaphor." In *Metaphor and Thought*, edited by Andrew Ortony, 19–41. Cambridge, UK: Cambridge University Press.

Bodenhausen, Galen V., and C. Neil Macrae. 1998. "Stereotype Activation and Inhibition." In *Advances in Social Cognition*, vol. 11, edited by Robert S. Wyer, Jr., 1–52. Mahwah, NJ: Erlbaum.

Bontekoe, Ron. 1987. "The Function of Metaphor." *Philosophy and Rhetoric* 20:209–26.

Bozeman, Barry. 2007. *Public Values and Public Interest: Counterbalancing Economic Individualism*. Washington, DC: Georgetown University Press.

———, Pamela N. Reed, and Patrick Scott. 1992. "Red Tape and Task Delays in Public and Private Organizations." *Administration & Society* 24.3:290–322.

Breton, Albert, and Ronald Wintrobe. 1985. *The Logic of Bureaucratic Conduct: An Economic Analysis of Competition, Exchange, and Efficiency in Private and Public Organizations*. New York: Cambridge University Press.

Camp, Elisabeth. 2005. *Josef Stern, Metaphor in Context*. Cambridge, MA: MIT Press, 2000. *Nous* 39.4:715–31.

Campbell, Joseph. 1968. *The Hero with a Thousand Faces*, 2nd ed. Princeton, NJ: Princeton University Press.

Cantalupo, Charles. 1988. "Hobbes's Use of Metaphor." *Restoration: Studies in English Literary Culture, 1660–1700* 12.1:20–32.

Chaiken, Shelly. 1980. "Heuristic versus Systematic Information Processing and the Use of Source versus Message Cues in Persuasion." *Journal of Personality and Social Psychology* 39:752–66.

Christensen, Robert K., Holly T. Goerdel, and Sean Nicholson-Crotty. 2011. "Management, Law, and the Pursuit of the Public Good in Public Administration." *Journal of Public Administration Research and Theory* 21.1:125–40.

Cornelissen, Joep P. 2002. "On the 'Organizational Identity' Metaphor." *British Journal of Management* 13:259–68.

Coyne, Richard D. 1995. *Designing Information Technology in the Postmodern Age: From Method to Metaphor*. Cambridge, MA: MIT Press.

Crossan, Mary M., Henry W. Lane, and Roderick E. White. 1999. "An Organizational Learning Framework: From Intuition to Institution." *Academy of Management Review* 24:522–37.

Dallek, Robert. 1984. *Ronald Reagan: The Politics of Symbolism*. Cambridge, MA: Harvard University Press.

Davidson, Donald. 1979 [1978]. "What Metaphors Mean." In *On Metaphor*, edited by Sheldon Sacks, 29–46. Chicago: University of Chicago Press.

deLeon, Linda, and Robert B. Denhardt. 2000. "The Political Theory of Reinvention." *Public Administration Review* 60.2:89–97.

Denhardt, Robert B., and Janet Vinzant Denhardt. 2000. "The New Public Service: Serving Rather Than Steering." *Public Administration Review* 60.6:549–59.

Dibella, Anthony J., Edwin C. Nevis, and Janet M. Gould. 1996. "Understanding Organizational Learning Capability." *Journal of Management Studies* 33:361–79.

Driver, Michela. 2002. "The Learning Organization: Foucauldian Gloom or Utopian Sunshine?" *Human Relations* 55:33–54.

Easterby-Smith, Mark. 1997. "Disciplines of Organizational Learning." *Human Relations* 50:1085–113.

Eco, Umberto. 1983. "The Scandal of Metaphor: Metaphorology and Semiotics." *Poetics Today* 4.2:217–57.

———. 1990. *The Limits of Interpretation*. Bloomington: Indiana University Press.

Edelman, Murray. 1971. *Politics as Symbolic Action*. Chicago: Marham Publishing Company.

Entman, Robert M. 2004. *Projections of Power: Framing News, Public Opinion, and U.S. Foreign Policy*. Chicago: University of Chicago Press.

Eubanks, Philip. 2000. *A War of Words in the Discourse on Trade: The Rhetorical Constitution of Metaphor*. Carbondale: Southern Illinois University Press.

Farazmand, Ali. 1989. "Crisis in the U.S. Administrative State." *Administration & Society* 21:173–99.

Fiol, C. Marlene, and Marjorie A. Lyles. 1985. "Organizational Learning." *Academy of Management Review* 10:803–14.

Fiske, Susan T., and Donald R. Kinder. 1981. "Involvement, Expertise and Schema Use: Evidence from Political Cognition." In *Personality, Cognition, and Social Interaction*, edited by Nancy Cantor and John F. Kihlstrom, 171–90. Hillsdale, NJ: L. Erlbaum Associates.

Fogelin, Robert J. 1988. *Figuratively Speaking*. New Haven, CT: Yale University Press.

Gibbs, Raymond W. Jr. 1992. "When Is Metaphor? The Idea of Understanding in Theories of Metaphor." *Poetics Today* 13:575–606.

Gilbert, Daniel T., and J. Gregory Hixon. 1991. "The Trouble of Thinking: Activation and Application of Stereotypic Beliefs." *Journal of Personality and Social Psychology* 60:509–17.

Gilbert, Scott F. 1979. "The Metaphorical Structuring of Social Perceptions." *Soundings* 62:166–86.

Hall, Richard H. 1968. "Professionalism and Bureaucratization." *American Sociological Review* 33:92–104.

Hausman, Carl R. 1989. *Metaphor and Art: Interactionism and Reference in the Verbal and Non-Verbal Arts*. Cambridge: Cambridge University Press.

Hendry, Chris. 1996. "Understanding and Creating Whole Organizational Change through Learning Theory." *Human Relations* 49:621–41.

Henle, Paul. 1958. *Language, Thought and Culture*. Ann Arbor: University of Michigan Press.

Henry, Nicholas. 2010. *Public Administration and Public Affairs*, 11th ed. New York: Pearson.

Hobbes, Thomas. 1996. *Leviathan*, edited by Richard Tuck. Cambridge, UK: Cambridge University Press.

Howe, Nicholas. 1988. "Metaphor in Contemporary American Political Discourse." *Metaphor & Symbolic Activity* 3:87–104.

Hubbell, Larry. 1990. "The Relevance of the Heroic Myths to Public Servants." *American Review of Public Administration* 20:139–54.

———. 1991a. "Ronald Reagan as Presidential Symbol Maker: The Federal Bureaucrat as Loafer, Incompetent Buffoon, Good Ole Boy, and Tyrant." *American Review of Public Administration* 21:237–53.

———. 1991b. "Heroes in the Public Service." *Administration & Society* 23:194–200.

Hume, David. 1955. *A Treatise of Human Nature*, edited by L. A. Selby-Bigge. Oxford: Clarendon Press.

Iyengar, Shanto. 1991. *Is Anyone Responsible? How Television Frames Political Issues.* Chicago: University of Chicago Press.

Jamieson, G. Harry. 1985. *Communication and Persuasion.* Beckenham, UK: Croom Helm Ltd.

Jankowicz, Devi. 2000. "From LO to 'Adaptive Organization'." *Management Learning* 31:470–90.

Jones, Matthew. 1990. "Organizational Learning: Collective Mind or Cognitivist Metaphor?" *Accounting, Management and Information Technology* 5:61–77.

Jørgensen, Torben Beck. 1999. "The Public Sector in an In-Between Time: Searching for New Public Values." *Public Administration* 77.3:565–84.

Katz, Albert N. 1992. "Psychological Studies in Metaphor Processing: Extensions to the Placement of Terms in Semantic Space." *Poetics Today* 13:607–32.

Kaufman, Herbert. 1977. *Red Tape: Its Origins, Uses, and Abuses.* Washington, DC: Brookings.

Kernaghan, Kenneth. 2003. "Integrating Values into Public Service: The Values Statement as Centerpiece." *Public Administration Review* 63.6:711–9.

Kettl, Donald F. 2000. "Public Administration at the Millennium: The State of the Field." *Journal of Public Administration Research and Theory* 10.1:7–34.

Kim, Daniel H. 1993. "The Link between Individual and Organizational Learning." *Sloan Management Review* 35:37–50.

Kinder, Donald R., and David O. Sears. 1985. "Public Opinion and Political Action." In *The Handbook of Social Psychology*, 3rd ed., edited by Gardener Lindzey and Elliot Aronson, 659–742. New York: Random House.

Kruglanski, Arie W., Martha Crenshaw, Jerrold M. Post, and Jeff Victoroff. 2007. "What Should This Fight be Called? Metaphors of Counterterrorism and Their Implications." *Psychological Science in the Public Interest* 8:97–133.

Lakoff, George. 1993. "The Contemporary Theory of Metaphor." In *Metaphor and Thought*, 2nd ed., edited by Andrew Ortony, 202–51. Cambridge, UK: Cambridge University Press.

———. 2004. *Don't Think of an Elephant: Know Your Values and Frame the Debate.* White River Junction, VT: Chelsea Green Publishing.

———, and Mark Johnson. 1980. *Metaphors We Live By.* Chicago: University of Chicago Press.

———, and Mark Johnson. 1999. *Philosophy in the Flesh: The Embodied Mind and Its Challenge to Western Thought.* New York: Basic Books.

Landau, Mark J., Brian P. Meier, and Lucas A. Keefer. 2010. "A Metaphor-Enriched Social Cognition." *Psychological Bulletin* 136:1045–67.

————, Daniel Sullivan, and Jeff Greenberg. 2009. "Evidence That Self-Relevant Motivations and Metaphoric Framing Interact to Influence Political and Social Issues." *Psychological Science* 20:1421–7.

Landau, Martin. 1972. *Political Theory and Political Science: Studies in the Methodology of Political Inquiry*. New York: Humanities Press.

Lane, Larry M., and James F. Wolf. 1990. *The Human Resources Crisis in the Public Sector*. New York: Quorum.

Locke, John. 1959. *An Essay Concerning Human Understanding*, edited by Alexander Campbell Fraser. New York: Dover.

Maasen, Sabine, and Peter Weingart. 2000. *Metaphors and the Dynamics of Knowledge*. London: Routledge.

Maesschalck, Jeroen. 2004. "The Impact of New Public Management Reforms on Public Servants' Ethics: Towards a Theory." *Public Administration* 82.2:465–89.

Mangham, Iain L. 1996. "Some Consequences of Taking Gareth Morgan Seriously." In *Metaphor and Organizations*, edited by David Grant and Cliff Oswick, 21–36. London: Sage.

March, James G., and Herbert A. Simon. 1958. *Organizations*. New York: Wiley.

McInerny, Ralph. 1968. *Studies in Analogy*. The Hague: Martinus Nijhoff.

McSwite, Orion C. 1997. *Legitimacy in Public Administration: A Discourse Analysis*. Thousand Oaks, CA: Sage Publications.

Menzel, Donald. 2003. "Public Administration as a Profession." *Public Integrity* 5.3:239–49.

Miller, Eugene. 1979. "Metaphor and Political Knowledge." *The American Political Science Review* 73.1:155–70.

Mio, Jeffrey Scott. 1996. "Metaphor, Politics, and Persuasion." In *Metaphor: Implications and Applications*, edited by Jeffrey Scott Mio and Albert N. Katz, 127–45. Mahwah, NJ: Erlbaum.

————. 1997. "Metaphor and Politics." *Metaphor and Symbol* 12:113–33.

————, Ronald E. Riggio, Shana Levin, and Renford Reese. 2005. "Presidential Leadership and Charisma: The Effects of Metaphor." *Leadership Quarterly* 16:287–94.

Mooij, Jan Joghann Albinn. 1976. *A Study of Metaphor*. Amsterdam: North-Holland.

Morgan, Gareth. 1980. "Paradigms, Metaphors and Puzzle Solving in Organizational Theory." *Administrative Science Quarterly* 25:605–22.

————. 1983. "More on Metaphor: Why We Cannot Control Tropes in Administrative Science." *Administrative Science Quarterly* 28:601–7.

————. 2006. *Images of Organization*, 2nd ed. [updated]. Beverly Hills, CA: Sage.

————. 2011. "Reflections on Images of Organization and Its Implications for Studies of Organization and Environment." *Organization & Environment* 24:459–78.

Newland, Chester A. 2003. "The Facilitative State, Political Executive Aggrandizement, and Public Service Challenges." *Administration & Society* 35.4:379–407.

Nonaka, Ikujiro. 1994. "A Dynamic Theory of Organizational Knowledge Creation." *Organization Science* 5:14–38.

————, and Hirotaka Takeuchi. 1995. *The Knowledge-Creating Company*. New York: Oxford University Press.

O'Brien, Gerald V. 2003. "Indigestible Food, Conquering Hordes, and Waste Materials: Metaphors of Immigrants and the Early Immigration Restriction Debate in the United States." *Metaphor and Symbol* 18:33–47.

Osborne, David, and Ted Gaebler. 1993. *Reinventing Government: How the Entrepreneurial Spirit Is Transforming the Public Sector*. New York: Penguin Books.

———, and Peter Plastrik. 1997. *Banishing Bureaucracy: The Five Strategies for Reinventing Government*. Reading, MA: Addison-Wesley Publishing Company, Inc.

Oswick, Cliff, Tom Keenoy, and David Grant. 2002. "Note: Metaphor and Analogical Reasoning in Organization Theory: Beyond Orthodoxy." *Academy of Management Review* 27:294–303.

Ottati, Victor, and Robert S. Wyer. 1993. "Affect and Political Judgment." In *Explorations in Political Psychology*, edited by Shanto Iyengar and William James McGuire, 296–320. Durham, NC: Duke University Press.

———, Susan Rhoads, and Arthur C. Graesser. 1999. "The Effect of Metaphor on Processing Style in a Persuasion Task: A Motivational Resonance Model." *Journal of Personality and Social Psychology* 77:688–97.

Pennington, Nancy, and Reid Hastie. 1986. "Evidence Evaluation in Complex Decision Making." *Journal of Personality and Social Psychology* 51:242–58.

Petty, Richard E., and John T. Cacioppo. 1986. "The Elaboration Likelihood Model of Persuasion." In *Advances in Experimental Social Psychology*, vol. 19, edited by Leonard Berkowitz, 123–205. New York: Academic Press.

Pinder, Craig C., and V. Warren Bourgeois. 1982. "Controlling Tropes in Administrative Science." *Administrative Science Quarterly* 27:641–52.

Putnam, Linda, and Suzanne Boys. 2006. "Revisiting Metaphors of Organizational Communication." In *The Sage Handbook of Organization Studies*, edited by Stewart R. Clegg, Cynthia Hardy, Tom Lawrence, and Walter R. Nord, 541–76. London: Sage.

Ricoeur, Paul. 1977. *The Rule of Metaphor*. Translated by Robert Czerny. Toronto: University of Toronto Press.

———. 1978 [1975]. *The Rule of Metaphor: Multi-Disciplinary Studies in the Creation of Meaning in Language*. Translated by Robert Czerny with Kathleen McLaughlin and John Costello. Toronto: University of Toronto Press.

Rosen, Bernard. 1983. "In the Public Interest." *The Bureaucrat* 12.4:41–3.

———. 1986. "Crises in the U.S. Civil Service." *Public Administration Review* 46:195–215.

Rosenbloom, David H. 1983. "Public Administration Theory and the Separation of Powers." *Public Administration Review* 43.3:219–27.

Sandelands, Lloyd E., and Ralph E. Stablein. 1987. "The Concept of Organization Mind." In *Research in the Sociology of Organizations*, edited by Samuel B. Bacharach and Nancy DiTomaso, 135–61. Greenwich, CT: JAI Press.

Schneider, Susan C., and Reinhard Angelmar. 1993. "Cognition in Organizational Analysis: Who's Minding the Store?" *Organization Studies* 14:347–75.

Schön, Donald A. 1979. "Generative Metaphor: A Perspective on Problem-Setting in Social Policy." In *Metaphor and Thought*, edited by Andrew Ortony, 254–83. Cambridge, UK: Cambridge University Press.

———. 1993. "Generative Metaphor: A Perspective on Problem Setting in Social Policy." In *Metaphor and Thought*, 2nd ed., edited by Andrew Ortony, 135–61. Cambridge, UK: Cambridge University Press.

Searle, John. 1983 [1969]. *Intentionality*. Cambridge: Cambridge University Press.

Shannon, Benny. 1992. "Metaphor: From Fixedness and Selection to Differentiation and Creation." *Poetics Today* 13:659–85.

Shen, Yeshayahu. 1997. "Metaphors and Conceptual Structure." *Poetics* 25:1–16.

Simon, Herbert A. 1991. "Bounded Rationality and Organizational Learning." *Organization Science* 2:125–34.

Snodgrass, Adrian, and Richard Coyne. 1992. "Models, Metaphors and the Hermeneutics of Designing." *Design Issues* 9.1:56–74.

Sopory, Pradeep, and James Price Dillard. 2002. "The Persuasive Effects of Metaphor: A Metaanalysis." *Human Communication Research* 28:382–419.

Stone, Deborah A. 1988. *Policy Paradox and Political Reason.* Glenview, IL: Scott Foresman & Co.

Stout, Margaret. 2007. "Bureaucrats, Entrepreneurs, and Stewards: Seeking Legitimacy in Contemporary Governance." Unpublished PhD dissertation, Arizona State University, Phoenix.

———. 2009. "Enhancing Professional Socialization through the Metaphor of Tradition." *Journal of Public Affairs Education* 15.3:289–316.

Taylor, Frederick Winslow. 1967. *The Principles of Scientific Management.* New York: Norton.

Terry, Larry D. 1997. "Public Administration and the Theater Metaphor: The Public Administrator as Villain, Hero, and Innocent Victim." *Public Administration Review* 1:53–61.

Thompson, Seth. 1996. "Politics without Metaphors Is Like a Fish Without Water." In *Metaphor: Implications and Applications*, edited by Jeffrey Scott Mio and Albert N. Katz, 185–201. Mahwah, NJ: Lawrence Erlbaum.

Tourangeau, Roger, and Robert J. Sternberg. 1982. "Understanding and Appreciating Metaphors." *Cognition* 11:203–44.

Tsoukas, Haridimos. 1991. "The Missing Link: A Transformational View of Metaphors in Organizational Science." *Academy of Management Review* 16:566–85.

van der Wal, Zeger, and Leo Huberts. 2008. "Value Solidity in Government and Business: Results of an Empirical Study on Public and Private Sector Values." *The American Review of Public Administration* 38.3:264–85.

Van Teeffelen, Toine. 1994. "Racism and Metaphor: The Palestinian—Israeli Conflict in Popular Literature." *Discourse and Society* 5.3:381–405.

Van Wart, Montgomery. 1998. *Changing Public Sector Values.* New York: Garland Publishing.

Vavrus, Mary Douglas. 2000. "From 'Women of the Year' to 'Soccer Moms': The Case of the Incredible Shrinking Women." *Political Communication* 17.2:193–213.

Walsh, James P. 1995. "Managerial and Organizational Cognition: Notes from a Trip Down Memory Lane." *Organization Science* 6:280–321.

———, and Gerardo Rivera Ungson. 1991. "Organizational Memory." *Academy of Management Review* 16:57–91.

Way, E. Cornell. 1994. *Knowledge Representation and Metaphor.* Oxford: Intellect.

Weber, Max. 1949. *The Methodology of the Social Sciences.* New York: The Free Press.

———. 1968. *Economy and Society: An Outline of Interpretive Sociology.* New York: Bedminster Press.

Weick, Karl E. 1989. "Theory Construction as Disciplined Imagination." *Academy of Management Review* 14:516–31.

Wildavsky, Aaron. 1988. "Ubiquitous Anomie: Public Service in an Era of Ideological Dissensus." *Public Administration Review* 48:753–5.

Wilson, Woodrow. 1887. "The Study of Administration." *Political Science Quarterly* 2.2:197–222.

———. 1966. *The Papers of Woodrow Wilson*, vol. 5. Princeton, NJ: Princeton University Press.

Wyer, Robert S., and Thomas K. Srull. 1989. *Memory and Cognition in Its Social Context.* Hillsdale, NJ: Erlbaum Associates.

4 Towards Sensory-based Strategy for Public Service Ethics

The present chapter draws on the synergies between Gadamer's notion of *Bildung* and sensory-based metaphors. The chapter provides a brief overview of metaphors and their hermeneutic relationship with understanding/*Bildung* and explores the implications for ethics management in the public service. The chapter places emphasis on the role of sensory experience as a source for metaphors engaged in a hermeneutical process of generating new understanding. We use the concept of felt-sense to denote the domain for sensory experience. By addressing the differences between sensation and perception, we discern the reflexive dimensions of sensual perception. We therefore need to describe the nature of sensual perception—what its component "parts" are and how it operates as a form of judgment, moral reasoning, and behavior, if we are to discover sensory-based practices for ethics management. More precisely, we investigate how sensual perception meets social, cultural, and moral order, thus compelling reflexive forms of sense-making by which people manage moral deliberation. Finally, we briefly expound on the application of sensory-based strategies in education and marketing.

A Hermeneutic Relationship between Metaphors and Understanding

In this book we suggest that metaphors are central to our ways of understanding. Snodgrass and Coyne (1992) outline the Greek origins of the word metaphor (*metaphora*), meaning transfer. According to Lakoff and Johnson (1980, 3): "Metaphor is pervasive in everyday life, not just in language but in thought and action. Our ordinary conceptual system, in terms of which we both think and act, is fundamentally metaphorical in nature." In their book *Metaphors We Live By*, they state that metaphors can create or lead to new understandings since they are capable of transforming one concept to another: "The essence of metaphor is understanding and experiencing one kind of thing in terms of another." (1980, 5) But how do metaphors structure our understanding? Johnson (Lakoff and Johnson 1999) illustrates this by reconstructing the phrase: "I see what you're saying". He reconstructs the sentence to its metaphorical source domain; that is, seeing while knowing the subject matter. Thus, seeing becomes correlated with knowing. Such correlation arises out of the embodied functioning in the world, where we regularly face cases in which seeing correlates with knowledge. Thus, the source domain of the metaphor emerges from the body's sensorimotor system.

When engaged in a hermeneutic process, metaphors function as prejudices, as noted by Gadamer, but can be changed and reveal multiple meanings and hence trigger the possibility of changing our understandings. (McClintock and Ison 1996) Understanding then emerges from an iteration between extrapolating our pre-understandings (or prejudices as described by Gadamer (2006 [1975])) and reflecting on and then revising these understandings: "Metaphors and models do not have static, one-off meanings, but are potentially capable of revealing multiple meanings, which can be progressively disclosed by the to-and-fro movement of the hermeneutic circle." (Snodgrass and Coyne 1992, 70) These pre-understandings pre-structure our experiences and are, in turn, revised by those experiences when engaged in a dialogic process. As a result, diverse understandings developed.

The role of metaphors in raising different understandings is an important methodological contribution to public servants' endeavor to work in a diverse stakeholder context in which policy actors exhibit differences in understanding, such as when managing public issues. Diversity among policy actors engaged in a policy-making process suggests many different metaphors are being used. As a source domain of metaphors that allows a way to appreciate different understandings in public service ethics, we use sensory experience embodied in the idea of "felt-sense".

Felt-Sense as a Sensory Domain for Metaphors

The felt-sense is the embodiment, namely bearing awareness inside the body, of one's sensory domain. The concept of felt-sense was developed by the American philosopher and psychotherapist Eugene Gendlin (1962 [1997]) as an approach to counseling that aims at encouraging people to raise their attention to their felt-sense of a situation, which is often referred to as "body awareness", "body knowing", or "body wisdom". Gendlin explains the meaning of felt-sense as:

> The soft underbelly of thought . . . a kind of bodily awareness that . . . can be used as a tool . . . a bodily awareness that . . . encompasses everything you feel and know about a given subject at a given time . . . It is felt in the body, yet it has meanings. It is body and mind before they are split apart.
>
> (Gendlin 1978, 33, 165)

In his studies, Gendlin observed that some people responded better than others in psychotherapeutic counseling since they were able to focus on a felt-sense of the problem with which they were faced. (Purton 2007) When studying such a phenomenon in depth, he developed methods for encouraging the practice of focusing as a way of improving the interaction between the flow of experiencing the client within the framework of understanding and respect. According to Gendlin:

> Today . . . [b]esides logical schemes and sense perception we have come to recognize that there is also a powerful felt dimension of experience that is prelogical, and that functions importantly in what we think, what we perceive, and how we behave . . . The task at hand is to examine the relationships between this felt dimension of experience and logical and objective orders . . . Meaning is formed in the interaction of experiencing and something that functions symbolically. Feeling without symbolization is blind; symbolization without feeling is empty . . . we cannot even know what a concept 'means' or use it meaningfully without the 'feel' of its meaning. No amount of symbols, definitions, and the like can be used in the place of the felt meaning.
>
> (Gendlin 1962 [1997], 1, 5)

Gendlin uses a broader understanding of "felt-sense" to include multiple levels of experience through the body such as sensing, hearing, reflecting. By developing the technique of felt-sensing that occurs in psychotherapy, Gendlin does not incline to privilege body knowing over intellectual knowing, yet he offers to integrate both sources of knowledge into holistic knowing:

> Gendlin's view is that our cultural history leads us into the temptation to ignore our bodies as sources of knowledge. We have a tendency to restrict knowing to the manipulations of the intellect . . . to ignore or suppress this awareness . . . [so that we are] unable to attend to the wisdom of the body.
>
> (Hay and Nye 2006 [1998], 70)

According to Gendlin (1984, 1996), felt-sense is a process that incorporates three main goals:

1. To capture and comprehend the client's experience;
2. To become conversant with means of interaction with the client as a part of a constructive process of mutual understanding;
3. To evaluate how the client might have felt once engaged in different modes of interaction.

Capturing and comprehending the client's experiencing means the possibility of an empathic feeling sensed through our own body that is similar to what the other is feeling in a given stage of the process, which enables the therapist to have a better understanding of the lived experience of the client. Once the psychotherapist captures the experiencing of the client in the modality of body empathy, the psychotherapist translates the client's felt-sense in terms of sounds, words, or bodily gestures. Finally, the psychotherapist must assure that he/she verifies whether the client learned how to find ways of symbolizing his/her experience.

The practice of felt-sense has also been developed in the field of spiritual education by making stronger links between spirituality and the felt-sense. (Hyde 2008a, 2008b) The felt-sense, it is being argued, is part of spirituality and as such it must be addressed in the spiritual education of children and young people. (Watson 2013)

Felt-Sense and Its Applications

Sensation and Perception as Components of the Felt-Sense Process

Sensation and perception are considered two main stages of processing felt-sense. Sensation occurs when the stimulus impinges on the receptor cells of a sensory organ, which is regarded as a biochemical (and neurological) response: "[S]ensation is the result of the activity of the psycho-physical organism, and is produced, not received . . . Sensation expresses the excitation, the stimulation of mind. It arouses the mind to put forth effort." (Dewey 1967 [1887], 43–4) Perception, on the other hand, originates from the Latin word *perceptio* or *percipio*, which means "evaluation with the mind or senses". Perception refers to the state of awareness or understanding of sensory information by the brain. The distinction between sensation and perceptions can be illustrated through speech. For newborn Japanese children, "l" and "r" are spelled out as distinct, while Japanese adults cannot make such distinction (sensation). This could be explained by the fact that Japanese adults are no longer able to make sense of the difference when speaking because it does not matter in their language. The Japanese adults' brains interpret (perception) both sounds as one so they are unable to hear the difference.

Vision is another sense that we can use to demonstrate the difference between sensation and perception. (Krishna 2008) In their research on perception biases, Raghubir and Krishna (1996) showed different judgments of space and distance traveled resulting from visual illusions. For example, the "direct distance" bias, whereby direct distance between the endpoints of non-straight lines of equal length influenced their perceived length, where the one with the shorter direct distance between endpoints is perceived to be shorter.

One of the applications of felt-sense can be clearly seen in the Sensory Marketing approach. Krishna (2013) defines Sensory Marketing as "marketing that engages the consumers' senses and affects their perception, judgment and behavior". The essence of the sensory marketing approach is the understanding that there can be more to a product than meets the eye and, in fact, also the ear, nose, mouth, or fingers. Many attributes of products are based on interactions between the senses and on the assumption that a product that appeals to the senses of the consumers, or to a combination of their senses, will be more seductive and therefore profitable. Moreover, a product that challenges the traditional sensations and would offer the consumers a new experience would also appeal to the public and, once again, turn the product profitable. An example of this would be a new texture of a familiar ice cream or a unique scent of a familiar shampoo.

Other unique examples can be found in a field such as Molecular Gastronomy, which transcends the traditional sense of taste and aims at appealing to other senses at the same time, including vision—providing glamourous and well-designed dishes, smell—offering new scents arising from unique ingredients, touch—relating to new and unexpected textures, etc. Many recent marketing strategies and efforts focus on developing new products with unique and sensory attributes. The most successful ones would be those that manage to offer the consumer a new and unexpected experience, either performing a familiar activity using the senses in a new way or a new activity activating the senses in an unprecedented manner.

In order to demonstrate how sensory marketing affects our senses we now move on to explore and discuss the five senses.

Application in Sensory Marketing

Vision

According to Krishna (2013), the majority of sensory marketing has until recently focused on the sense of sight, based on the prevalence of this sense over the others. Moreover, the sense of sight is also considered to be of crucial importance for activities normally associated with the other senses. That is, that the sense of sight facilitates, although it does not otherwise limit, the possibility to identify sources of sound, to experience textures, or to explore new tastes.

In terms of marketing, it is also important to know the mechanism of the sense of sight in order to best use it for marketing reasons, as well as for operating optical illusions and/or biases aimed at enhancing a certain sale. The first use of visual sensory marketing is visual signatures often used by companies in order to identify themselves in a visual manner and create certain memorable dependence in the minds of the consumers. This would be the case for companies' logos, e.g., the partially eaten apple representing the Apple brand, or the designed letter M standing for the McDonalds brand, or the case of repeated use of a particular color in order to identify it with the brand, e.g., the color pink for the fight against breast cancer, or the colors red and black placed together reminding the consumer of the Coca-Cola brand.

This last example is defined as Color Psychology. (Singh 2006) According to this approach, 62 percent–90 percent of the personal assessment of a certain product is based on color alone, which highlights the prevalence of the sense of sight for marketing purposes. Moreover, it has been found that colors hold the ability to influence a person's moods and attitudes, and therefore the strategic use of color can go beyond its mere aesthetic value; it can alter the customers' mood, can increase or decrease their appetite, manipulate perception of time, etc. It is important to note, however, that just as much as it could ameliorate the customers' experience, it can also decrease it, which all marketing teams should take into consideration.

Another important component of visual marketing is the use of color in order to create a recognizable experience and develop dependence between a particular color and a product or a cause. We have previously mentioned the color pink traditionally used for the fight against breast cancer, a link that is so strongly branded that oftentimes when encountering the color a person would instinctively think of this specific cause even if the product is not related to it. Another social cause related with color would be the social revolution in Iran in 2009 in which protesters demanded the removal of President Mahmoud Ahmadinejad. The repeated use of the color green during the protests, televised appearances, and social media was so clear that nowadays the entire campaign is better known as the "Iranian Green Movement".

Visual marketing can also make use of illusions and biases for marketing reasons. Krishna defines bias as "any consistent misalignment between sensation and perception". (2013, 29) The above mentioned distinction between sensation and perception is especially important with regard to visual marketing as the two are used very differently for marketing reasons and their marketing effects might even contradict. The gap between sensation and perception is obvious in many examples, such as the sizing bias where one can make a product seem bigger or smaller based on its surroundings, e.g., placing a drink in a tall or short glass would change the perception of quantity, or, for instance, the recent tendency of several supermarkets to provide larger shopping carts in order for the products inside to seem very few. Another bias would be the Direct Distance bias, manipulating the way a person would perceive the distance from one point to another, making it seem shorter or longer even if the actual distance is either the same or the opposite from that perceived. For marketing purposes, this would affect desired store locations within shopping centers or the way a certain shop would choose to place its products in relation to the entrance, the cashiers, or even a specific item of interest in the shop.

Smell

At a glance, the importance and significance non-Western countries relate to scent goes far beyond the importance, or lack of thereof, given to smell in Western societies. Some would even consider smell as the most undervalued of all the senses. (Krishna 2013) It seems clear then that the society one grows up in can be very important in shaping our scent preferences. This, however, does not go to say that our scent preferences cannot be shaped throughout the years. (Krishna 2013)

Maybe more than other senses, the sense of smell is particularly personal, while scent sensation varies with personal as well as social and cultural experiences. According to Krishna (2013), peoples' opinions on different scents are influenced by their background. For instance, smell is typically related with memory, a link we will later develop in terms of ethical conduct. Therefore, oftentimes the very intimate and personal smell of "home" accompanies the individual wherever they go and would cause the sensation of "throwback" when encountered in a different context. Similarly, smell can have cultural meaning. For instance, for the residents of the Andaman Islands off the shores of India the entire yearly calendar is based on the odors of flowers blooming at different times during the year, each season being named after a specific odor. (Classen, Howes, and Synnott 1994)

Different cultures can also interpret odors in different ways, e.g., for the people of the Dogon tribe in Mali, the most attractive scent for a young man or woman would be the smell of onion, while the same population in Western societies would be warned against this same smell in case they wish to encounter a person from the opposite sex. Another example would be the smell of cows, which is considered to be the most attractive one to wear for the people of the Dassanech ethnic group in Ethiopia, a scent that is highly disregarded in Western cultures. (Fox 2009)

The personal and cultural attributes of the sense of smell are particularly important for marketing purposes. Certainly, venders in different areas of the world must know their audience and adjust the scent of their products to the local perception of smell. For instance, while the smell of a new car is considered to be desired in Western cultures, it is considered to be unpleasant in China. Therefore, vendors in the United States should enhance this smell while vendors in China should try to mask it with more desired scents in order to promote the sale. Scents can also be used for marketing purposes in order to attract the customers' attention, e.g., when the TV series "Weeds" published an advertisement in a magazine with a marijuana scent strip attached, attracting the readers' attention and relating to the content of the series; or in order to convey a message, e.g., when a political candidate sent the voters a pamphlet with a garbage-scented strip attached, relating to negative comments regarding other candidates.

Other marketing uses would include perfuming shops in order to create a more pleasant atmosphere and keeping the clients in the shop for as long as possible, or attaching smells to giveaways and souvenirs at hotels, sites, or restaurants as a tool to remind the customers of the positive experience they had even long after they leave. (Krishna 2013) The current challenge in terms of olfactory marketing would be the ability to transmit scent through the Internet or on TV. A growing part of the population purchases more and more using the Internet or simply goes online or watches TV and is being exposed to different types of advertisements. However, the above-mentioned commercial potential of the sense of smell cannot be met, as there is no known method to transmit scent through digitized means and this needs to be mimicked by visual and auditory means instead.

Taste

Taste is personal, dependent on experience. That is to say that the experience of taste, i.e., the ability to tell if a certain food in tasty or not, assumes the person has already had the experience of tasting it. Unlike the sense of sight or smell, taste does not happen instinctively or passively, if you will, but rather demands the individual to be active in tasting in order to say if the sensory experience has been more or less positive.

Due to this unique attribute of the sense of taste, and until one tries a certain food and can testify regarding its taste, the other senses serve as substitutes for the sense of taste and can even be considered as components of it. (Krishna 2013) When faced with a new dish and long before the sense of taste comes into action, the visual presentation of the dish, as well as its aroma, and sometimes even the physical location of the client in the restaurant and the music playing in the background, play important roles in its evaluation. Viewed this way, it seems

> Taste as we know it is less of a sense by itself and more of an amalgamation of all our senses . . . The combination and juxtaposition of colors and textures is not to be ignored either; usually, a dish is crafted in consideration of all of its sensory properties.
>
> (Krishna 2013, 106)

This is also pertinent when it comes to sensory marketing aiming at the sense of taste. Since the sense of taste is often better understood and reached using the other senses, this gives companies the possibility to reach for those senses in order to enhance sales. Therefore, marketing efforts will not turn towards manipulating the taste itself, rather amending and manipulating packaging, portions, layout, etc., in order to appeal to an amalgamation of senses and therefore affect the psychological aspects of the sense of taste. Krishna (2013) offers the example of labeling of packages as "small", even without there being less substance, which would generate an increase in sales as people would rather feel as though they have eaten less or healthier. Another example would be the layout of yogurt packages in a variety of flavors rather than a unique flavor that had been proved to sell less.

Other factors appealing to the taste of a certain product would be the odor in the restaurant or coffee shop, e.g., Starbucks has been emphasizing the smell of coffee in their shops, which has improved the customers' tasting experience. The tasting experience is also improved when adding uniqueness, e.g., when Starbucks renamed their coffee sizes in order to appear "foreign" and more exotic than the regular small-medium-large sizes, or when a certain restaurant serves in uniquely shaped plates and glasses, which adds both to the aesthetics as well as to the culinary experience. This is highly noticeable with regard to unique cooking methods, which unnecessarily make the food taste better, however, certainly making it more unique and desired; such is the case with molecular cuisine or with traditional cooking that buries the food in the ground.

These characteristics of the sense of taste make it multisensory and, as such, it obliges the individual to sharpen the other senses in order to fully appreciate a certain taste. This could be considered a liability in terms of marketing; however, we would choose to look at it as an opportunity for companies to offer a multisensory experience and challenge the way products are being treated prior to being served or sold.

Touch

As previously mentioned, many of the senses embody an intimate experience, be it a certain smell relating to a personal memory or the experience of a taste varying according to personal preferences. However, the most intimate sense of them all is the sense of touch, often relating to emotions of sympathy, affection, and love between people maintaining a certain relationship—romantic, familial, friendly, or professional. According to Krishna (2013), the sense of touch, or haptics, exists passively on all parts of our body as haptic receptors are located on all external parts of the body and even in some internal locations such as in the mouth. Therefore, the sense of touch is not limited to one specific area in the human body and haptic sensation can be identified even without the help of any other sense.

The primary attributes of objects identified through the sense of touch are hardness, texture, temperature, and weight. All of these four attributes, among others, relate to marketing and can be incorporated in consumer products, foods, textiles and footwear, electric devices, etc. An example of this would be in the form of a perfume bottle, proved to sell more once the design was in the form of a woman's torso, attracting the eye of potential clients. Another example would be the association of smooth textures with feminine clothing while masculine clothing would be associated with rougher textile textures. (Krishna 2013) In the latter example the sense of touch joins the sense of sight (and possibly also the sense of hearing if music was playing in the store and the sense of smell is a certain scent used for marketing purposes) in order to create a full sensory experience.

Another example of the difference made by a physical sensory experience is the use of touchscreen smartphones or tablets. By using the screen itself and managing the device using nothing but the fingertips, the human-product interaction is being altered, making it much more personal and engaging. The mere name of this technology—touchscreen—suggests the innovation in these types of devices connecting the natural haptic experience and the device. It is therefore noticeable that the way a certain product "feels" may change the way we perceive it and consequently increase or decrease the sale of these products. Sophisticated marketers would not wait until the consumer has had the haptic experience of the product and would incorporate it in the advertisement itself, e.g., the brand StoveTop has launched a bus shelter campaign where the ad itself releases heat in wintertime. This way the customers are happy with the product even before they have purchased it, which increases the chances of them purchasing it later on. In terms of human touching, it has been proved that a waitress lightly touching the customers can make significantly more money in tips.

Hearing/Audition

The sensory experience of hearing is yet another passive human sense that allows the individual to integrate into his/her surroundings and better communicate with it. For instance, hearing allows us to be aware of road dangers, to participate in a human communication (even without speaking), or to enjoy music as a pastime. The sense of hearing is best related to the notion of orientation—it allows the person to orient him- or herself within a certain space, while oftentimes people whose hearing is impaired sense spatial disorientation to a certain degree and are disconnected from their surroundings. (Mattox and Simmons 1977)

In marketing we mainly focus on music as a pastime, while it has been proven that a pleasant consumer hearing experience helps in increasing sales or improving the general consumer experience. However, all marketers should note that the choice of music should not be incidental but adjusted to the target audience, the environment, and other sounds arising from it as well as the type of location or given situation. (Krishna 2013) For instance, the music playing in the background of a car commercial might be significantly different than the music played in a baby food commercial. The same with locations—a clothing store would most probably play a different type of music than that played at a Michelin restaurant.

Many large companies use sounds as part of their branding efforts, creating sounds identifiable with their brand. This would be the case for the lion roar for the MGM studios brand or the start sound of an Intel computer. These sounds, when encountered outside of their specific context, would still make us think of the brand or picture its logo in our minds, which participates in the brand recognition process. Such audible attributes also relate to speaking—for instance, a deep masculine voice would more often be associated with authority and confidence, and thus often used for voiceovers of bank commercials or news companies. However, it is found that a higher pitched feminine voice increases sales, although this is still subject to contradicting studies. (Krishna 2013)

Sounds play a major role in marketing even without us noticing it—music can be found as a waiting sound on the phone, in the elevator leading to the company's office, in the radio or TV commercial of the product, and as ambient sound in the store. A conjunction between these different sounds would strengthen the brand and allow better recognition for the customers. Some would even go as far as forming partnerships with certain music companies or artists to be recognized with the brand while their music is being played in the company's locations, in order to strengthen the brand once again and give it a younger and more updated flair. (Krishna 2013) All these efforts go to show the importance of music for marketing purposes and the ability of music to affect the customer's experience and increase, or decrease, sales.

Applying Felt-Sense in Customer Judgment and Behavior

As indicated in the overview, touching, tasting, hearing, smelling, and seeing a product play an important role in our understanding and hence affect our buying behavior. (Krishna 2012) Perception of the roles played by the five senses has become recognized in the field of marketing and customer behavior. (Achrol and Kotler 2012) Sensory marketing applies an understanding of sensation and perception as it concerns consumer behavior. The role of sensory experience in judging and deciding impacts important factors influencing customers' buying experience, store environment, time spent in the store, shopping satisfaction, satisfaction with a product or service, pleasure seeking, consumer decision-making styles, and the level of interest of the consumer. (Haghigi, Saeed, and Kyanoush 2011; Krishna and Schwarz 2014)

The idea behind sensory marketing is to use the unconscious sensory stimuli as an effective way to engage consumers and affect their perception: "Marketing that engages the consumers' senses and affects their behaviors." (Krishna 2010, 2) It is suggested that once all the five senses are brought together in harmony, they exert a high stimulating power and therefore achieve greater effect on the customer. (Hultén 2013) As seen above, many shops use various environmental stimuli such as sight (color and space), sound (music), smell (odor), and touch (smoothness, temperature) in order to create a memorable experience for the consumer and potentially affect their future behavior. (de Farias, Aguiar, and Sales 2014)

In the present era, sensory experience should be applied in order to build a long-term relationship with the consumer. (Krishna, Lwin, and Morrin 2010) For that, communication devices apply sensory-based marketing strategies to maintain a memorable sensory experience that gives the consumer opportunities to perceive and experience the product and services. (Heitzler, Asbury, and Kusner 2008)

Applying Felt-Sense in Public Service Ethics

In order to allow public administrators to provide the holistic ethical public service expected of them, we suggest a hermeneutic sensory-based strategy to enhance professional development and ethical judgment of public servants. We argue that the role of sensory experience in ethical decision-making entails "felt-sense", which involves the human senses of the individual, which, in turn, affect his perception, judgment, and behavior. (Krishna 2012; Waskul and Vannini 2008)

The suggested sensory approach is based on the belief that for a public servant to reach the most appropriate ethical decision, he or she must rely on their natural human senses and engage in sensory experience while facing moral dilemmas or employing the written code of conduct. This shows that what is considered to be reflexive and natural behavior, such as the instantaneous reaction of the senses, can transcend beyond the personal sphere onto the public sphere. Sensory judgments are value judgments that have seemingly "immediate" and potent somatic importance. (Classen, Howes, and Synnott 1994, 16)

It is within this framework that we suggest that the sensory-based metaphors can be drawn hermeneutically to allow public servants to promote ethical standards and conduct in the public service while employing methods of understanding. In our view, metaphors embodied in the sensorimotor domain may give rich expression to public values and extend beyond codified ethical principles and standards towards values of Practical Wisdom. By doing so, and this would be our main contribution, ethics management in the public service can be strengthened by drawing upon sensory-metaphors to the fullest and will, in practice, make sense of the ethics in the public administration.

Bibliography

Achrol, Ravi S., and Philip Kotler. 2012. "Frontiers of the Marketing Paradigm in the Third Millennium." *Journal of the Academy of Marketing Science* 40.1:35–52.

Classen, Constance, David Howes, and Anthony Synnott. 1994. *Aroma: The Cultural History of Smell.* New York: Routledge.

de Farias, Salomão Alencar, Edvan Cruz Aguiar, and Francisco Vicente Sales. 2014. "Store Atmospherics and Experiential Marketing: A Conceptual Frame Work and Research Propositions for an Extraordinary Customer Experience." *International Business Research* 7.2:87–99.

Dewey, John. 1967 [1887]. *John Dewey: The Early Works 1882–1898*, vol. 2, edited by Herbert W. Schneider. Carbondale, IL: Southern Illinois University Press.

Fox, Kate. 2009. "The Smell Report." *Social Issues Research Centre.* http://www.wierook.nl/docs/smell.pdf

Gadamer, Hans-Georg. 2006 [1975]. *Truth and Vethod*, 2nd ed. New York: Continuum.

Gendlin, Eugene. 1962 [1997]. *Experiencing and the Creation of Meaning.* Evanston, IL: Northwestern University Press.

———. 1978. *Focusing.* New York: Everest House.

————. 1984. "The Client's Client: The Edge of Awareness." In *Client-Centered Therapy and the Person-Centered Approach*, edited by Ronald F. Levant and John M. Shlien, 212–241. New York: Praeger.

————. 1996. *Focusing-Oriented Psychotherapy: A Manual of the Experiential Method*. New York: Guilford Press.

Haghigi, M., Nia H. Saeidnia, and Ghavin G. H. Kyanoush. 2011. "The Role of Emotional Satisfaction in Customers' Behavioral Intentions Regarding Service Quality in the Hotel Industry." *Journal of Marketing Management* 6.12:45–62.

Hay, David, and Rebecca Nye. 2006 [1998]. *The Spirit of the Child*, rev. ed. London: Jessica Kingsley.

Heitzler, Carrie D., Lori D. Asbury, and Stella L. Kusner. 2008. "Bringing 'Play' to Life: The Use of Experiential Marketing in the VERB™ Campaign." *American Journal of Preventive Medicine* 34.6:188–93.

Hultén, Bertil. 2013. "Sensory Cues as In-Store Innovations: Their Impact on Shopper Approaches and Touch Behavior." *Journal of Innovation Management* 1.1:17–37.

Hyde, Brendan. 2008a. *Children and Spirituality: Searching for Meaning and Connectedness*. London: Jessica Kingsley.

————. 2008b. "The Identification of Four Characteristics of Children's Spirituality in Australian Catholic Primary Schools." *International Journal of Children's Spirituality* 13.2:117–27.

Krishna, Aradhna. 2008. "Spatial Perception Research: An Integrative Review of Length, Area, Volume, and Number Perception." In *Visual Marketing: From Attention to Action*, edited by Michel Wedel and Rik Pieters, 167–92. New York: Erlbaum.

————. 2010. *Sensory Marketing: Research on the Sensuality of Products*. New York: Routledge.

————. 2012. "An Integrative Review of Sensory Marketing: Engaging the Senses to Affect Perception, Judgment and Behavior." *Journal of Consumer Psychology* 22.3:332–51.

————. 2013. *Customer Sense: How the 5 Senses Influence Buying Behavior*. Basingstoke, UK: Palgrave Macmillan.

————, May O. Lwin, and Maureen Morrin. 2010. "Product Scent and Memory." *Journal of Consumer Research* 37.1:57–67.

————, and Norbert Schwarz. 2014. "Sensory Marketing, Embodiment, and Grounded Cognition: A Review and Introduction." *Journal of Consumer Psychology* 24.2:159–68.

Lakoff, George, and Mark Johnson. 1980. *Metaphors We Live By*. Chicago: University of Chicago Press.

————. 1999. *Philosophy in the Flesh: The Embodied Mind and Its Challenge to Western Thought*. New York: Basic Books.

Mattox, Douglas E., and F. Blair Simmons. 1977. "Natural History of Sudden Sensorineural Hearing Loss." *Annals of Otology, Rhinology & Laryngology* 86.4:463–80.

McClintock, David, and Ray Ison. 1996. "Responsible (Response-Able) Design Metaphors." In *Accounting for Ourselves, Proceedings of World Congress 3 on Action Learning, Action Research and Process Management*, edited by David McClintock and Ray Ison, 146–9. Bath, UK: University of Bath.

Purton, Campbell. 2007. *The Focusing-Oriented Counselling Primer*. Ross-on-Wye: PCCS Books.

Raghubir, Priya, and Aradhna Krishna. 1996. "As the Crow Flies: Bias in Consumers' Map-Based Distance Judgments." *The Journal of Consumer Research* 23:26–39.

Singh, Satyendra. 2006. "Impact of Color on Marketing." *Management Decision* 44.6:783–9.

Snodgrass, Adrian, and Richard Coyne. 1992. "Models, Metaphors and the Hermeneutics of Designing." *Design Issues* 9.1:56–74.

Waskul, Dennis D., and Phillip Vannini. 2008. "Smell, Odor, and Somatic Work: Sense-Making and Sensory Management." *Social Psychology Quarterly* 71:53–71.

Watson, Jacqueline. 2013. "Knowing Through the Felt-Sense: A Gesture of Openness to the Other." *International Journal of Children's Spirituality* 18.1:118–30.

5   Sight

In this chapter we investigate the moral sense of seeing and foreseeing, analyzing and considering policies and their plausible consequences. This entails the ability and the need for public servants to foresee the implications and consequences of public policies on the diverse layers of the population. Being the representatives of the public interest, public servants must "know their audience" and think strategically and flexibly when implementing policies of any sort and, if needed, bring the public's concerns to the attention of decision-makers.

The History and Science of Sight

Visual perception begins with visible light gained through photoreceptors called cones and rods located in the retina (which lines the back of the eye). These two types of receptors receive incidental light due to their highly specialized shape and optical capacities. (Franze et al. 2007) Light encompasses the small part of the electromagnetic spectrum that we can sense with the human eye. Both cones and rods go through the process of dark adaptation; however, the cones are more responsible for the perception of color while the rods are responsible for brightness.

The visual information processing occurs in non-sensory cortex centers that are important in the perception and recognition of objects. (Leopold and Logothetis 1999) Although most information processing occurs in these cortex centers, less is known about the exact processing procedure for a single visual image. Several studies in humans of conscious visual perception prove that some areas of the brain are involved in neural activity. Yet, it is still unclear exactly how the joint neural network that functions to selectively integrate visual events contributes to generating conscious perception. (Farbiszewski and Kranc 2012)

The sense of sight appears to be imbued with mystical, theological influences. The story of Exodus begins with God's appearance to Moses in the midst of the Burning Bush:

> And the angel of the LORD appeared unto him in a flame of fire out of the midst of a bush: and he looked, and, behold, the bush burned with

fire, and the bush was not consumed. And Moses said, I will now turn aside, and see this great sight, why the bush is not burnt.

(Exodus 3:2–3)

God's use of the burning bush to make his appearance to Moses was not aimed at getting Moses' attention, but rather to denote that God is transcendent—nothing like other beings. Such a glorious vision of God is meant to show that God's being remains unknown. (Murray 1964, 10; Ryan 2014)

Sight has been recognized by philosophical and empirical thinkers as an appealing field of research that deals with perception and perceptual experience. Themes such as color visualization, spectrum inversion, the waterfall illusion, blindness, all have raised philosophical investigations about perception and image or appearance. (O'Callaghan 2008)

Ancient Greek studies influenced modern scientists who developed theories of color. The ancient Greek philosophers actually raised the connection between seeing and truth (associated with evidence). Thucydides, the ancient political philosopher who founded "scientific history" based on evidence-gathering, demonstrated this link by suggesting that factual history is that based on the authority of sight (*autopsia*) and not on hearsay or on memory distortion and lies. (Bloch 2008) Plato and Aristotle provided us with the way the theories of vision and the concept of light in particular intertwine with general theories on science and logical reasoning. Plato contributed to the study of vision by asserting that vision is subject to many types of errors, so that color is not a characteristic of an object nor does it depend on the observer:

> Then it will be apparent that black or white or any other color whatsoever is the result of the impact of the eye upon the appropriate motion, and therefore that which we call color will be in each instance neither that which impinges nor that which us impinged upon, but something between, which has occurred, peculiar to each individual. Or would you maintain that each color appears to a dog, or any other animal you please, just as it does to you?

(Plato 153–4)

Aristotle chooses to focus on the transparency of the medium required to actualize colors. According to Aristotle, "Sense is that which is receptive of the form of sensible objects without the matter." (Aristotle *On the Soul*, II, 424a,19) The eye represents the external world, thus enabling the sense of sight to perceive it. In the beginning of the *Metaphysics*, Aristotle elevates sight over the other senses: "We prefer sight, generally speaking, to all other senses. The reason for this is that, of all the senses, sight best helps us to know things, and reveals many distinctions." (Aristotle *Metaphysics A*, 980a25)

If we turn to the meaning of the sense of vision as looking at, viewing, or contemplating, we can see that theory and practice in the public service are already interrelated, requiring public servants' concerted and long-term efforts of attention in daily practices that identify and build structures of value in the light of ideals of professional excellence. The moral force behind the requirement for *looking* is based on the relation between sight and truth, as developed by ancient philosophers, since people are almost compelled by what they *can* see. Thus, virtue depends on vision. Virtue consists in seeking for, seeing the goodness in others:

> But I would suggest that, at the level of serious common sense and of an ordinary non-philosophical reflection about the nature of morals, it is perfectly obvious that goodness is connected with knowledge; not with impersonal quasi-scientific knowledge of the ordinary world, whatever that may be, but with a refined and honest perception of what is really the case, a patient and just discernment and exploration of what confronts one, which is the result not simply of opening one's eyes but of a certain and perfectly familiar kind of moral discipline.
>
> (Murdoch 1997, 330)

Iris Murdoch (1970, 36–7) summarizes this connection and process by using the concept of "attention":

> Do we really have to choose between an image of total freedom and an image of total determinism? Can we not give a more balanced and illuminating account of the matter? I suggest we can if we simply introduce into the picture the idea of attention, or looking, of which I was speaking above. I can only choose within the world I can see, in the moral sense of "see" which implies that clear vision is a result of moral imagination and moral effort.

Attention is defined as a form of contemplation. This process of thinking allows opening up one's mind to seeing another person as an individual, worthy of regard—in the sense of observant attention. Murdoch (1970, 19) gives the example about the inner progress of a mother in her feelings toward her daughter-in-law whom she dislikes. Over time, the mother decides to look again at her daughter-in-law and learn other dimensions of her personality. In summarizing the change in how the mother looks at her daughter-in-law, Murdoch claims that "M has in the interim been *active*, she has been *doing* something" [her emphases].

Based on Murdoch's work, we would argue that paying attention is a sub-activity of seeing, as without the latter the first would not exist. However, while seeing can be categorized as a passive motion, paying attention would be the active interpretation of it. Seeing is indeed a natural and instinctive action; we do not put much effort into it, if any at all, and only by following the instinct of opening our eyes would we see. However, once paying attention to something, one is truly seeing, looking into, acknowledging. Unlike seeing, paying attention requires being active. The main difference we can identify between the two is by employing a certain level of judgment—as one would choose to pay attention to something another would disregard. And vice versa, one might completely disregard and categorize as meaningless something another would consider to be of extreme importance.

Attention seeking requires the exercise of moral imagination that can lead to reinterpretation of a given situation. This implies that seeing the situation in more ethical terms can alter one's actions and take a deliberate stance towards the encounter with a situation, with truth. This internal process entails an ethical decision-making process that occurs instinctively and subconsciously. We rarely choose what to pay attention to at a first glance, and sometimes it is only though another person's judgment that one would pay attention to something they would not have done spontaneously. Applying moral judgment would generate attention to certain things over others; one would certainly notice things they would consider as unethical, corrupt, morally wrong, or unjust. Interestingly, we would notice wrongdoings more than we would actions we would consider as ethical. In this sense, seeing goes beyond the passive motion of opening the eyes and regarding, but rather judging, appreciating, analyzing, and reflecting.

It is important to note that the things we pay attention to, our moral judgments, may vary from one culture to another, with time passing by and with the various life experiences one would go through. Moral imagination is not by chance a very intimate and personal experience that could dramatically differ from one person to another, taking into account multiple factors such as culture, age, gender, marital status, profession, education, and financial and social status. Seeing in this sense would be the perception each and every one of us holds on many issues and on many occasions; the way one perceives a certain given situation shapes it and internalizes it.

This does not go to say one cannot change their perceptions using those of others. In other words, it occurs quite frequently that an insight drawn from another person's perception "opens the eyes" of another, thus changing the first person's perception, allowing them to see things in a different manner and from a different point of view. It is a familiar notion when one feels they have gone through an "eye opening experience", referring to an experience that has shaped their perception differently than it was before and has allowed them to see similar things in a different manner.

The use of sensorial metaphor relating to the sense of sight is no accident, as this is the sense of sight, which is instinctively correlated with moral imagination and perception. According to Lakoff and Johnson (1999, 46), defined as Primary Metaphors are metaphors that "arise naturally, automatically and unconsciously through everyday experiences by means of conflation, during which cross-domain associations are formed . . . Universal early experiences lead to universal conflations, which then develop into universal (or widespread) conventional conceptual metaphors". This would lead us to consider seeing as understanding or knowing, vision as the sensorimotor domain of the subjective judgment of knowledge. We therefore consider getting our knowledge, as subjective as it may be, through the action of seeing and reflecting upon what we have seen.

Moral imagination is not to be taken lightly, as it shapes one's entire life perception and therefore the way they would regard their life experiences, relations with others, successes, failures, goals, desires, and many more. Our moral imagination would also inevitably affect the actions one would choose to take in life and the way one would go about dealing with every given situation with which they are faced.

We want to establish here what we mean by the notion of moral imagination to flesh out its use in the process of ethical deliberation. Moral imagination in terms of foresight is defined as "The ability to imaginatively discern various possibilities for acting within a given situation to envision the potential help and harm that are likely to result from a given action." (Johnson 1993, 202)

Traditional views of moral imagination are found in the work of Kant. For Kant, imagination cannot play any role in moral judgment since "its cultivation is at best a luxury, at worst a danger". (Kant 1979, 140) However, John Dewey addressed a new role for imagination in pragmatic thinking. For pragmatism, imagination is seen as the capacity to understand the actual in the light of the possible. (Alexander 1993, 371) Dewey identifies two ways to practice moral imagination. The first form is empathy as direct responsiveness to others which is "the animating mold of moral judgement". (Dewey 1974, LW 7:270) This form means that one should go beyond himself and his interests by imagining himself as the other and sympathizing with his needs, interests, and concerns. The second way in which we transform our understanding of a given situation is by going beyond the existing limits of our convictions and commitments that prevent us from *seeing* the wider picture.

Moral imagination is a necessary but not sufficient condition for moral deliberation. Werhane's (1999) innovative research on moral imagination found that both individuals and organizations make poor decisions by not being consciously aware of the limitations of existing mental models. Moral imagination is the capacity to challenge mental models in order to reframe ethical dilemmas and realize new solutions. The process of moral imagination results in transforming existing ways of thinking and operating.

Werhane developed a stagist model of applying moral imagination in ethical decision-making. The first stage, called reproductive imagination, involves raising awareness of the contextual factors that affect perception of moral dilemma:

> (a) Awareness of one's context, (b) Awareness of the script or schema functioning in that context, and (c) Awareness of possible moral conflicts or dilemmas that might arise in that context, that is, dilemmas created at least in part by the dominating script.
>
> (1994, 21–2)

The second stage, productive imagination, dealing with the need to reframe an ethical dilemma from different perspectives: "consists in revamping one's schema to take into account new possibilities within the scope of one's situation and/or within one's role." (Werhane 1994, 22) The third stage, creative imagination or free reflection, leads to the development of morally agreeable options to solve the problem:

> (a) the ability to envision and actualize possibilities that are not context-dependent but encouraged by or project a fresh schema, and/or (b) the ability to envision possibilities that other reasonable persons could envision. Morally imaginative free play also includes (c) evaluation: (i) envisioning how morally to justify actualizing these possibilities and/or (ii) how to evaluate both the status quo and these newly formulated outcomes.
>
> (Werhane 1994, 85)

Werhane brings several cases in which managers who insisted on following fixed ways of solving ethical issues raised in their organizations have failed to use moral imagination, which could help to overcome organizational misdeeds. Werhane argues that "Some individuals and institutions are trapped in a framework of history, organization, culture and tradition . . . a framework that they often allow to drive their decision-making to preclude taking into account moral concerns." (1994, 3) Werhane explains such prevailing patterns:

> Our conceptual schemes function in a variety of ways. In selecting, focusing, framing, organizing and ordering what we experience they bracket and leave out data, and emotional and motivational foci taint or color experience. These conceptual schemes are constantly under the influence of new social and cultural stimuli, hence they are subject to change. Now and again, however, our perspectives become narrow, microscopic or even fantasy-driven, or a particular point of view becomes ingrained so that one begins to adopt only that perspective.
>
> (1994, 9)

In the following we will make clear how these general conceptualizations of each stage provide a compelling basis for the ethical training required for public administrators.

Entering the twenty-first century, design of a moral imagination program still involves complex sets of skills, traits, and capacities that can be attained and articulated in multiple ways. (Narvaez et al. 2006) They suggest using film clips in the character education curriculum, which allows addressing contextual factors involved in ethical decision-making instead of relying on schematic interpretations listed in codes of ethics. This method of moral imagination education based on sight-sensory strategy is employed through group discussion of the film and group activities that engage the public servant in forming a moral perspective regarding the ethical dilemma in question.

A key component in the film method is the use of an inductive educational tool following the viewing of the film. Induction centers the subject on the feelings of the observed other—whether in a film or in a role play. After each film clip is shown, the instructor asks a series of questions concerning the context that affects perception of a moral dilemma and the moral perspectives of the characters presented in the film. By raising questions such as "How do the characters feel in the situation they are in?" and "What do you think affects that character's thinking and behavior?", the group members are invited to take on the roles of the characters in the film, thereby encouraging perspective taking by the participants. An additional activity after the film discussion is role play that requires participants to switch roles so that they will be exposed to the characters' different approaches.

Role play is used as a strategy to teach values but also to alter views of social justice or determine who warrants moral concern (Flay and Allred 2003) as well as a technique for exercising prosocial skills and putting values into action. (Caplan et al. 1992) Role play allows the subject to imagine himself in the situation of the other and gives the subject direct access to become familiar with the thoughts and emotions one experiences in a given dilemma.

The advantage of both film and role play techniques is that they allow cognitive distance since it is not actual experience in developing empathy towards those who warrant moral concern. The rationale behind the use of film technique is that it provides the participant an experience of another's state of mind through viewing a film, an opportunity for the participant to consider the values and concerns involved in the moral dilemma. It is then instructive to discuss the emotions and values of the character on the screen, especially if the discussion helps the participant to consider whether he or she has ever been in a similar dilemma. In addition, at the last phase of the moral imagination training program, the instructor asks what the participants might have done if they found themselves in a similar situation, with the hope of coming up with innovative solutions and possibilities.

This theoretical framework of a wider interpretation of sight in the decision-making process and in interpersonal relations can be translated into an actual professional strategy. In the following analysis we aim at offering a Visual Strategy in the Public Administration, where public servants could, and sometimes should, widen their perspective in order to really see the public and foresee policy implications. Using the sensorial experience of seeing and its metaphorical interpretations, public servants would sharpen their ethical consideration and would exercise their moral imagination capacities for the public benefit.

Visual Strategy for Ethics Management in the Public Administration

As mentioned above, Werhane (1999) divides the method of applying moral imagination in ethical decision-making into several stages. In the Reproductive Imagination stage, she discusses raising awareness of the contextual factors that affect perception of moral dilemma. Extended into the Public Administration sphere, this would refer to the predisposed knowledge and experience public servants have with regard to: (1) the public they aim to serve; its unique characteristics, needs, limitations, and desires. This would require a high level of professionalism and years of experience on the part of public servants. (2) The policies at hand pertinent to the specific role they play within the public administration. All public servants operate within a limited framework defined by policies, and their practical effects in the form of laws, regulations, jurisdictions, etc. Each public servant knows the policies within which he must operate and their implications on the public; the set of ground rules he/she is expected to maintain and promote.

Werhane also related moral imagination to awareness of possible moral conflicts or dilemmas that might arise. Within the public administration context, this would refer to the expertise some public administrators hold, combining a high level of professionalism together with the wisdom gained over time, allowing them to not only know their public's characteristics and needs but also be able to foresee any potential needs in the future. Similar to other professional scenarios, experience over time and the aspiration to provide the best possible service would enable public servants to anticipate requests, needs, and even trends within the public. If these entail potential negative effects, a professional public servant should be able to foresee them and sometimes offer a remedy even before they arise. It is important to note, however, that this is not always possible and does not necessarily imply unprofessionalism on the part of public servants.

This awareness is also related to the assumption that experienced public servants should be able to foresee possible future policies, considering the professional expertise they hold, or changing professional practices. It is obvious certain policies are permanent and would not change as they incarnate the basic democratic values, although the means by which these policies are attained might vary. Thus, new regulations might arise, as well as new policy guidelines or recommendations. On a side note, changes in this character can be extremely beneficial to upholding the democratic values in changing times. One might also consider the required awareness of public servants to be their ability to foresee potential policy changes considering the political environment and its dynamics. All this would be considered to be the "inside information" public servants have access to, whereas the general public is only exposed to partial information, oftentimes when policies are already in place.

The second stage according to Werhane is Productive Imagination, where one is expected to reframe ethical dilemmas from different perspectives, taking into account new possibilities within the scope of one's situation. When faced with an ethical dilemma originating from the gap between the public's needs and current policies, or potential future policies, public servants must also regard the bigger picture. This would entail reframing the way they considered the situation beforehand and looking for the potential benefit that could come out of the new situation, both for the public itself or parts of it, as well as for the general public system. It would hardly be possible to have policies in place that are beneficial for the totality of the public, while at the same time allowing the bureaucratic system to maintain and promote it. Therefore, at this stage public servants should conduct a reanalysis of the given scenario, consider its advantages and disadvantages for the entire public they serve, while considering the options at hand. It might just be that the change underway might generate a bigger satisfaction by the public; this is yet to be disclosed. While using their inner information as well as professional expertise, public servants should go through this process before proceeding.

The third and final stage according to Werhane would be Creative Imagination or Free Reflection, which leads to the development of morally agreeable options to solve the problem. It is not enough to be able to see the public and know its needs, or being able to foresee potential ethical dilemmas that might occur. The exact level of expertise as well as the dynamics of the public service can be evaluated by its ability to solve ethical dilemmas or conflicting moral questions, if possible even before they arise; however, this is very rarely possible. Solving an ethical dilemma in the Public Administration would often require prioritization or the re-evaluation of current priorities. As previously mentioned, it would be extremely difficult to satisfy all parts of the society; however, the decision-making process must remain ethical and morally just. Oftentimes the prioritization of policies is a task for political decision-makers; however, public servants do have leverage in this regard when applying current policies and/or preparing new policies to be implemented. Once again, we refer to those "street-level bureaucrats" acting as an extension of the decision-making level, reaching the public and acting as a transmitter of information to all bureaucratic and political levels in order to maintain an ethical framework for the totality of the public.

When considering possible solutions to moral dilemmas, a certain level of sensibility should be implied. This sensibility in the public administration would rely on an intimate understanding of both the public's requests and the bureaucratic limitations, while aiming at reaching the *juste milieu* between the two. This technique would be comprised of morally seeing, imagining, and foreseeing for all public servants involved, together with the cooperation of the decision-making level.

Policies are often strict and unamendable. However, a true public servant knows how to adjust the policy at hand to the public, using this exact sensitivity and expertise acquired throughout the years. This does not go to say such adjustment would be possible at all times; however, the mere effort on the part of the public servants can sometimes bring remedy in itself. Seeing the public in the ethical sense enables public servants to be willing to go "the extra mile" in order to provide a quasi-personalized policy, allowing each and every person to reach their full potential while contributing back to the society as a whole.

Another interesting interpretation of Sight in the ethical sense would be based on the Visual Ethics theory. This ethnographic and anthropological approach, mainly drawn from visual arts such as painting, sculpture, photography, and motion pictures, claims our moral formation to be conceived based on the aesthetic experiences we collect. The Visual Ethics theory creates a clear connection between aesthetics and ethics. (Bucar 2016) This refers not only to the way one would perceive a certain situation, but rather the way the situation is being portrayed to them. In the visual arts, artists can choose the way they wish to portray their works and can therefore alter the way these would be perceived by the audience. The choice of constructing a particular visual in a particular way may have very important consequences, which, in turn, can be the object of the art itself. (Kienzler 1997)

When applied to everyday life, visual ethics can relate to the way different situations and scenarios are being presented as means to manipulate how these situations would be perceived. Taken one step further, when relating to the Public Administration, this would signify the way both policies and public needs are being portrayed to the public servants, be it a visual graph of policy goals, a picture taken from a disaster-hit area, a film made by representatives of the public, a document presenting an individual's financial condition, etc. The way these are portrayed would necessarily affect the moral imagination of the public servant and, consequently, his/her actions. This is where the ethical component plays a critical role; looks can deceive and therefore be used unethically in order to reach desired goals.

Such a visual ethical manipulation is also present with misleading or missing content of the story told. This is especially pertinent to public servants dealing with the public itself, meeting the people and offering them aid within the framework of the public administration. According to Kienzler: "When information is withheld or presented in such a way as to lead to slanted conclusions, then the concept of informed opinion, critical to ethical communication, is violated." (1997, 176) This also occurs with manipulated numbers, inconsistent reports, misleading graphs, unethical editing, and other visual aids that are unethically manipulated to suit a certain goal.

From this we advise that, conscious of these potential maneuvers and ethical visual manipulations, public servants should not proceed to any moral imagination or metaphorical perception before evaluating the ethical value of the visual elements with which they are faced.

In conclusion, far from being limited to the mere physical meaning of the sense of sight, the metaphorical meaning of this sense is certainly significant and central in the field of ethics in the Public Administration. Public servants should be able to "see" the public, in the sense of knowing them and acquiring professional experience in dealing with the public's needs and desires, while being able to foresee future needs and obstacles they may encounter. On the other hand, public servants should also be conscious of the policies and bureaucratic limitations at hand, while employing moral imagination in order to find the *juste milieu* between the public's needs and the administrative response. Seeing goes beyond the mere physical visualization, and extends to the individual's entire perception of life, his/her goals, aspirations, and challenges. When opening our eyes we do much more than looking, while morally and ethically judging the situations we are faced with and are accordingly inclined to act. In this sense, what you see is no longer what you get, but rather "the way you see is the way you act".

Bibliography

Alexander, Thomas M. 1993. "John Dewey and the Moral Imagination: Beyond Putnam and Rorty Toward a Postmodern Ethics." *Transactions of the Charles S. Peirce Society* 29.2:369–400.

Aristotle. 1907. "Introduction and Notes." In *De Anima*. Translated by Robert Drew Hicks. Cambridge: Cambridge University Press.

———. 1924. *Aristotle's Metaphysics*, edited by William David Ross. Oxford: Clarendon Press.

Bloch, Maurice. 2008. "Truth and Sight: Generalizing without Universalizing." *Journal of the Royal Anthropological Institute* 14:S22–32.

Bucar, Elizabeth M. 2016. "The Ethics of Visual Culture." *Journal of Religious Ethics* 44.1:7–16.

Caplan, Marlene, Roger P. Weissberg, Jacqueline S. Grober, Patricia J. Sivo, Katherine Grady, and Carole Jacoby. 1992. "Social Competence Promotion with Inner-City and Suburban Young Adolescents: Effects on Social Adjustment and Alcohol Use." *Journal of Consulting and Clinical Psychology* 60.1:56–63.

Dewey, John. 1974. *The Collected Works*, edited by Jo Ann Boydston. Carbondale, IL: SIU Press. Indicated by series (Early works EW, Middle Works MW, Later Works LW).

Farbiszewski, Ryszard, and Robert Kranc. 2012. "Receptors Sight Sense Genesis Eye Lens Transparency." *Progress in Health Sciences* 2.1:142–6.

Flay, Brian R., and Carol G. Allred. 2003. "Long-Term Effects of the Positive Action Program." *American Journal of Health Behavior* 27.Suppl 1:S6–21.

Franze, Kristian, Jens Grosche, Serguei N. Skatchkov, Stefan Schinkinger, Christian Foja, Detlev Schild, Ortud Uckermann, Kort Travis, Andreas Reichenbach, and Jochen Guck. 2007. "Muller Cells Are Living Optical Fibers in the Vertebrate Retina." *Proceedings of the National Academy of Sciences U S A* 104.20:8287–92.

Johnson, Mark. 1993. *Moral Imagination*. Chicago: University of Chicago Press.

Kant, Immanuel. 1979. *Lectures on Ethics*. Translated by Louis Infield. Indianapolis, IN: Hackett Publishing Company.

Kienzler, Donna S. 1997. "Visual Ethics." *Journal of Business Communication* 34.2: 171–87.

Lakoff, George, and Mark Johnson. 1999. *Philosophy in the Flesh: The Embodied Mind and Its Challenge to Western Thought*. New York: Basic Books.

Leopold, David A., and Nikos K. Logothetis. 1999. "Multistable, Phenomenon Changing Views in Perception." *Trends in Cognitive Sciences* 3.7:254–64.

Murdoch, Iris. 1970. *The Sovereignty of Good.* Abingdon, UK: Routledge.

———. 1997. *Existentialists and Mystics: Writings on Philosophy and Literature*, edited by Peter Conradi. London, UK: Penguin Books.

Murray, John C. 1964. *The Problem of God.* New Haven, CT: Yale University Press.

Narvaez, Darcia, Tracy Gleason, Christyan Mitchell, and Jennifer Bentley. 2006. "Integrative Ethical Education." In *Handbook of Moral Development*, edited by Melanie Killen and Judith G. Smetana, 703–35. Mahwah, NJ: Lawrence Erlbaum Associates.

O'Callaghan, Casey. 2008. "Seeing What You Hear: Cross-Model Illusions and Perception." *Philosophical Issues* 18.1:316–38.

Plato. 1973. *Theaetetus.* Translated by John McDowell. Oxford: Clarendon Press.

Ryan, Tom. 2014. "Our Pathway to God: Sight." *Compass* 48.4:14–20.

Werhane, Patricia. 1994. *Moral Imagination and the Search for Ethical Decision-Making in Management.* The Ruffin Lectures in Business Ethics. Charlottesville, VA: The Darden School, University of Virginia.

———. 1999. *Moral Imagination and Management Decision-Making.* New York: Oxford University Press.

6 Hearing

Hearing will be interpreted as the obligation relative to public servants to remain attentive to their surroundings, putting oneself in the place of the other in a hermeneutic manner, while being aware of one's own bias. By internalizing the needs and requests of the public and truly listening to their voice, public servants will better communicate with their communities and be able to provide a better, more suitable, and ethical public service.

The History and Science of Audition

The sense of hearing or Audition concerns our ability to perceive sound waves or vibrations through the ear over time. Sounds are among the objects we hear. Auditory experience is expressed through sounds, while sounds are viewed as intentional objects of audition. (Crane 2009) It is appropriate to note that whenever one hears something, they hear a sound. In other words, no one can hear anything without hearing a sound. Sounds are arguably included among the immediate objects of audition.[1]

The ability to hear sounds is limited for human beings as humans are only able to hear sound within the range of 20–20,000 Hertz. Animals' hearing range goes beyond that of humans; for example, dogs' hearing spectrum can reach the level of 40,000 Hertz. (Cutnell and Johnson 1998) Fetuses develop their sense of hearing during pregnancy by listening to their mothers' heartbeats. Once they are born, babies are able to differentiate between sounds in their closer environment, and by the age of two months, most babies recognize familiar voices and make vowel sounds. (Birnholz and Benecerraf 1983)

It is important to note that there is a difference between hearing and listening. Hearing is the way we perceive sound, while listening is what occurs when we choose to pay attention to the meaning of what we hear. To this we can add the Sound symbolism, which is the concept that hypothesizes the relationship between sound and meaning.

Philosophical studies of auditory perception raise certain challenges. (Maclachlan 1989; Matthen 2010; Noë 2004; Nudds 2001; O'Callaghan 2007) One set of challenges concerns the ontology of sounds, that is, what kinds of objects are sounds, and what audible qualities do sounds have? For instance, are sounds secondary qualities, waves, or some type of event-involving? In contrast to vision, for instance, hearing involves indirect awareness of sensations as sounds resulting from interactions of material objects and thus are experienced as independent of them or located in some direction at a distance. (O'Callaghan 2007) A sound is unlike a table. A sound results or takes place through time and space so it needs time and location to occur or unfold. Indeed, the identities of some common sounds are tied to patterns of change through time. For example, the sound of an ambulance siren is different from that of a police siren due to different patterns of qualitative change during their duration. The sound of the spoken word "team" is different from that of "meat" because we perceive their common set of audible qualities in a different temporal pattern. (Casati and Dokic 2005; Matthen 2010; O'Callaghan 2007; Scruton 1997)

Since the beginning of the modern era and onwards, the prevailing idea concerning sound is that sounds are secondary or sensory properties. (Noë 2004) Given their classification as immediate objects of audition that require no mediators for audition perception, sounds were grouped together with other perceptible proprieties such as colors, smells, and tastes. (Nudds 2001; O'Callaghan 2007) However, some scholars rejected property theories that held such an approach and instead suggested that sounds are not properties or qualities, but rather are individuals or particulars such as pitch, timbre, and loudness. (O'Callaghan 2007) According to O'Callaghan, sounds have time and spatial durations individuated in terms of the proprieties they display through time. Following O'Callaghan's account of sounds, other philosophers have suggested to identify sounds as events of an object's vibration. Scruton (1997) offers a theory of events of sounds based on the independence of sounds from their sources. Scruton's approach can be demonstrated by focusing on the auditory perceptual experience when listening to music. According to Scruton (1997), it is possible to reach auditory experience whose content includes merely sounds but not sound sources.

The dispute over the ontology of sounds, whether they are properties or individuals, leads to the discussion of the content of auditory experience, which is classified into three categories. The first group includes views that presuppose that we are able to hear only sounds and their qualities, such as pitch, timbre, loudness, duration, and location. The second holds a more permissive view that implies that we might be able to hear both sounds and their sources. The third group holds that we are able to hear objects beyond sounds and their sources, such as how the object is located in the environment. In short, such typology of theories of sounds and sources has become a fertile field for both metaphysical and psychological inquiries into auditory experience content.

Hearing as a Sensorial Strategy for Ethics Management in the Public Service

When applying the metaphor of hearing to the public administration, we would call for all public servants to engage in attentiveness to the public. This attentiveness would require differentiating between Hearing and

Listening, as mentioned above. While Hearing is a passive activity that does not require any action by the individual, Listening goes beyond remaining passive and merely acknowledging someone's needs. It can be categorized into two distinct types of action:

(1) The intentional activity of paying attention and fully understanding not only the verbal expression but also grasping the emotional aspect of what is being said. An individual being able to do this would be considered a "Good listener". Pence and Vickery (2012, 159) define good listening as a capacity that "entails the active involvement of an interlocutor who is attempting to understand what the other is feeling". We would therefore add a mental and emotional component to what could have been considered the merely physical activity of listening. We would argue public servants must also engage emotionally and not only intellectually, in order to provide a more ethical and thus professional public service. This would be termed by us as the "Empathic public servants".

(2) Listening in the public service would also entail acting on the things that have been said. We would incorporate within the definition of Listening, in contrast to hearing, the way in which something said becomes the direct reason for action. Listening is not only understanding or sympathizing with the interlocutor, but also allowing it to develop and ripen into an action. For example, in the public administration context, an individual seeking assistance from a certain public entity would express his or her needs verbally, which would then become the direct cause of a certain action. Listening is therefore seen as a tool, a catalyzer, and an incentive to go on and pursue action on the public administrator's part. De facto, this would mean "going the extra mile" when the standardized action no longer suffices. We would relate to the concept of "Administrative Responsiveness" (Stivers 1994) in this sense.

The Empathic Public Administrator

In this book we aspire to incorporate the idea of empathy in the public administration. It is suggested that "good listening" implies empathic capacities. Listening defined by active and emotional involvement on the part of the listener during a given interaction is what we can call active-empathic listening. (Bodie 2011) Empathic listening is viewed as a process whereby the listener puts himself or herself in the other person's place throughout.

Empathy is defined both as a "trait" and as a "process". (Duan and Hill 1996; Kennett 2002; Rogers 1975) Empathy consists of three dimensions, (Brems 2001) including 1) the ability to sense what the other person is experiencing from his inner experience, 2) the ability to remain open to another's experience and views with compassion and tolerance, and 3) the process of interacting to create an emotional bond. Empathy is central for effective listening since it "perceive[s] the internal frame of reference of another with accuracy and with the emotional components and meanings which pertain thereto as if one were the person, but without ever losing the 'as if' conditions." (Rogers 1959, 210–1) Applying empathy in listening creates an environment of open communication and helps the listener become more responsive and negotiate more effectively. (Bodie 2012)

We should note, however, that there is a limitation to the empathy a public servant can and should manifest towards their interlocutor. As per the hermeneutic approach, one should be able to understand and relate to another in order to have a clearer perception of reality. This while keeping in mind their own bias and remaining attentive to the role they themselves play in the relationship. As described by Gadamer (2006 [1975]), philosophical hermeneutics is described as the voice of another, thus relating back to the sense of hearing and the need to listen, while remaining aware of one's own bias yet not limited by it. When applied to ethics in the public administration, we would claim this requires of public servants to listen truly to their interlocutor, remaining open to exceeding their own bias, and considering the situation from a different and new perspective, while keeping in mind their own role and obligations. De facto, we could describe this as going as far as possible to assist an individual based on an emotional connection, within the limitation of not harming any other individual or underestimating existing rules and regulations. In other words, stretching the existing framework while keeping it intact as much as possible.

While it may sound instinctive and natural to express empathy towards one's interlocutor, it is not necessarily the case when it comes to the highly bureaucratic public administration. In these conditions, what does it truly mean to be an Empathic Public Administrator?

First, public servants should develop their empathic sensing to be able to "read between the lines" and identify more precisely citizens' concerns and needs. Because of this, they are more likely to become aware of potential difficulties and drawbacks at the initial stage of the policy implementation process and better able to anticipate objections. This would also make them more apt to lead a change to the policy implementation process and, in more rare yet possible occasions, lead a change in the policy-making process. Empathic listening is promoted by using a comfortable tone and allowing time and opportunity for the other person to share their doubts and concerns from a place of mutual respect.

Second, public servants must remain open-minded. As an empathic listener, public servants must be open to hear new perspectives, new solutions, and new possibilities, whether they themselves might agree with them or not. For that they need to suspend judgment and hold their criticism. This is not an easy task on both the personal and professional levels. On the personal level, all human beings are being led by their inherent values and psychological, cultural, and moral biases, while on the professional level, professional education and training relies on core guiding principles, which are not easily altered.

Last, public servants must develop their listening capacity in relating new incoming information by paraphrasing key points. An empathic listener demands clarifications or asks further questions about ambiguous or unclear issues, and encourages citizens to expand their concerns, while inviting reflection and thoughtful response. In order to identify common concerns or experiences of segments of the public, administrators must ask questions (Frederickson 1997), and we would add—listen to the answer. Public administrators should therefore avoid "broad questions" and focus on "narrow questions" in order to acquire the information needed to assess the quality and effectiveness of administrative performance.

Administrative Responsiveness

In public administration ethics, audition as a sensory experience is revealed through the idea of Administrative Responsiveness. (Stivers 1994) By introducing and highlighting the idea of responsiveness, Stivers claims too much emphasis has been put on public administrators' need to be responsible, relying heavily on the bureaucratic institutions, to the detriment of their responsiveness. This latter seems to be underestimated at best and considered to harm effectiveness and democratic accountability in the public service at worst. Some would even qualify responsiveness as on the verge of corruption, as it takes into account the personal aspect, of both the demanding and the responding types, putting significant weight on the interpersonal relations created in the process.

In shedding light on the importance of listening in the public administration, we would agree with Stivers (1994, 367) in claiming that "The practice of skillful listening can help administrators evolve toward a form of responsiveness that supports both democratic accountability and administrative effectiveness." This responsiveness would lead to a more open and respectful public administration, which would certainly contribute to regaining the public trust in the State's institutions and agencies.

According to Stivers, listening should be treated as a moral capacity for the practice of responsiveness in the public service. The capacity of listening motivates openness, respect for diverse viewpoints, reciprocity, and the potential for genuine dialogue. Within the context of public administration, listening is important because it helps administrators gather relevant information, identify situations and barriers to implementing policy decisions making more mindfully, and facilitate just and sensible judgment and actions.

By adding the empathy component to the responsiveness presented by Stivers, we believe that public administrators can become more accessible and relatable for the public; two traits that have become more and more distant from the perception of the public administration in the past two decades. Combined with empathy, responsiveness in the public administration would imply genuinely listening to citizens, stakeholders, superiors, and political entities. The entire relationship with and within the public administration could become more engaging and reciprocal, a place where interactions are no longer one-sided or perceived in "black and white" only. Listening enables unfolding the complexities of human interactions and encourages joint efforts of all sides involved in order to untangle them.

Methods for Promoting Listening in the Public Administration

In order for the public administration to listen carefully and remain attentive and responsive to the public's needs, a few methods can be put in place. A distinction should be made between two occasions during which the public interest is heard: the first would be when the administration is being reached by the public in an institutionalized-bureaucratic manner, e.g., request for permit renewals or approaching a governmental office with a specific request. The second would be at the initiative of the public service in order to become better acquainted with the entire public and listen to their needs and requests.

In the first scenario the methods for listening to the public are set in place or at least should be set and clear to the public in every democratic State. The tasks and areas of responsibility of each ministry or public agency should be clear, as well as the direct means to reach the relevant public servant in charge of the requested issue. A high level of transparency is critical in this sense, in order to enhance accessibility, allowing the citizens to approach whichever service they need and make their voice heard. This is where transparency, efficacy, and responsiveness all reunite and are pertinent whether the "listening mechanism" is at the initiative of the citizens or the public administration. On the flip side, lack of transparency and efficacy would naturally lead to lack of responsiveness and, in extreme cases, could even compromise the core democratic values of the administration.

Recent technological developments allow for a much easier and more accurate analysis of the public interest in a variety of issues, combined with more traditional methods of reaching out to the public and inviting them to express their will. The common use of websites and emails allows the public to reach out to the administration with questions, requests, and/or special demands. This is certainly the case in Western countries where the public administration has managed to keep up with technological advancements. We would therefore argue that all democratic regimes should adopt such communication manners with the public, letting go of the more traditional methods such as appointments and letters, which at best would delay the reaction time and prevent the public from making itself heard as quickly and as effectively. It is important to note, however, that for specific cases, where a more complex issue is at hand, the public service should maintain an interpersonal approach where an empathic public administrator could listen and assist to the best of his or her ability.

In the second scenario also, where the initiative is on behalf of the public administration reaching out to the public, technology has gone a long way in allowing the administration to listen to the public's needs. This would consist of websites encouraging the public to express their opinions, polls being conducted online on specific issues, invitations to write emails to governmental agencies, online feedback forms, and many more. Each and every method used is another step in an active engagement on the part of the public administration with the public, in order to listen and adjust or create services to better suit the public's needs. Once again, the engagement with the public, the will to genuinely listen to its needs, as well as the actual change it may lead in the public service not only ameliorates the service provided, but also creates a stronger bond between the administration and the public itself. Faced with the clear lack of trust in the public mechanism, which the New Public Management theory seeks to resolve among other things, this renewed bond created through listening might just offer a real solution.

It seems to us that the most important aspect of listening in ethical conduct in the public administration is an activity often disregarded. While it is important to remain attentive and responsive to the voices of the public, it would seem even more important to actively look out for the voices that are unheard. It is the public servants' responsibility to identify occasions in which the public's voice is not heard and work tirelessly to remedy it. This might occur regarding a specific issue, where the voices of the public are being over-shadowed by political or personal interests. This would go against any ethical standards in the public service, meant to respond to the public interest and provide the best and most ethical public service.

Public administrators would also have to make sure they hear ALL the voices of the public before moving to action. It is very common for those in positions of power and influence to be more easily heard by the decision-makers and implementers, affecting the public administration. In this case the public administration risks disregarding those whose voices are not being heard due to lack of accessibility, leadership, or political or economic capital. It is precisely these voices that are often in most need of public attention that are less heard and often outweighed by more influential voices. In ethical terms, public servants should not have any interest in mind other than the public one, unlike political figures who might have political considerations to be taken into account when choosing which voice to hear. Involving the public administration in this mindset would be no less than corrupting it and shattering the core values of an ethical public administration.

We would therefore argue that this is the task of the public administrators, to remain attentive not only to the content of what they hear from the public, but also to make sure they are presented with the entire picture composed of all the different interests and voices. In order to do so the public administration cannot stay passive awaiting the voices, but rather should be active in looking for the often underrepresented and unheard voices, while unveiling their needs and taking them into consideration.

Once all voices have been heard, it is the last task of the public administrators to ensure equal voice to all, thus not favoring any voice over any other for any reason. Public servants should ensure equal rights and opportunities to all citizens with no discrimination, allowing multiple perspectives in an environment free from any prejudice and regardless of sex, gender, race, class, ethnicity, religion, and disability. This goes to say that the tone of the voice or the identity of the one behind it should not affect the way change is being made; it is, however, only the content and the professional discretion of the public servant that are of crucial effect. For that, everyone's voice should be given a fair hearing; as mentioned by Stivers (1994), respect occurs only when we allow voices to be heard and to resonate.

Note

1. It should be noted that such conviction is debatable. For example, according to Sorensen (2007), we are able to hear silence, which does not engage with hearing any sound.

Bibliography

Birnholz, Jason C., and Beryl R. Benecerraf. 1983. "The Development of Human Fetal Hearing." *Science* 222:516–8.

Bodie, Graham D. 2011. "The Active-Empathic Listening Scale (AELS): Conceptualization and Evidence of Validity within the Interpersonal Domain." *Communication Quarterly* 59:277–95.

———. 2012. "Listening as Positive Communication." In *The Positive Side of Interpersonal Communication*, edited by Thomas J. Socha and Margaret Jane Pitts, 109–25. New York: Peter Lang.

Brems, Christiane. 2001. "Dimensionality of Empathy and Its Correlates." *The Journal of Psychology* 123:329–37.

Casati, Roberto, and Jerome Dokic. 2005. "Sounds." In *The Stanford Encyclopedia of Philosophy*, edited by Edward N. Zalta. http://plato.stanford.edu/archives/fall2005/entries/sounds/

Crane, Tim. 2009. "Intentionalism." In *Oxford Handbook of Philosophy of Mind*, edited by Brian McLaughlin, Ansgar Beckermann, and Sven Walter, 474–94. Oxford, UK: Oxford University Press.

Cutnell, John D., and Kenneth W. Johnson. 1998. *Physics*, 4th ed. New York: Wiley.

Duan, Changming, and Clara E. Hill. 1996. "The Current State of Empathy Research." *Journal of Counseling Psychology* 43:261–74.

Frederickson, H. George. 1997. *The Spirit of Public Administration*. San Francisco, CA: Jossey-Bass.

Gadamer, Hans-Georg. 2006 [1975]. *Truth and Method*, 2nd ed. New York: Continuum.

Kennett, Jeanette. 2002. "Autism, Empathy and Moral Agency." *The Philosophical Quarterly* 50:340–57.

Maclachlan, D. L. C. 1989. *Philosophy of Perception*. Englewood Cliffs, NJ: Prentice Hall.

Matthen, Mohan. 2010. "On the Diversity of Auditory Objects." *Review of Philosophy and Psychology* 1:63–89.

Noë, Alva, ed. 2004. *Action in Perception*. Cambridge, MA: MIT Press.

Nudds, Matthew. 2001. "Experiencing the Production of Sounds." *European Journal of Philosophy* 9:210–29.

O'Callaghan, Casey. 2007. *Sounds: A Philosophical Theory*. Oxford, UK: Oxford University Press.

Pence, Michelle E., and Andrea J. Vickery. 2012. "The Roles of Personality and Trait Emotional Intelligence in the Active-Empathic Listening Process: Evidence form Correlational and Regression Analyses." *International Journal of Listening* 26.3:158–74.

Rogers, Carl R. 1959. "A Theory of Therapy, Personality, and Interpersonal Relations, as Developed in the Client-Centered Framework." In *Psychology: A Study of a Science*, vol. 3, edited by Sigmund Koch, 184–256. New York: McGraw-Hill.

———. 1975. "Empathic: An Unappreciated Way of Being." *The Counseling Psychologist* 5:2–10 (Reprinted in Carl Ransom Rogers. 1980. *A Way of Being*, 137–64. Boston: Houghton Mifflin).

Scruton, Roger. 1997. *The Aesthetics of Music*. Oxford, UK: Oxford University Press.

Sorensen, Roy. 2007. *Seeing Dark Things*. Oxford, UK: Oxford University Press.

Stivers, Camilla. 1994. "The Listening Bureaucrat: Responsiveness in Public Administration." *Public Administration Review* 54:364–9.

7 Smell

Smell triggers personal and institutional memory, which is a key for quality public service. It is vital for public servants to regard the broader perspective of their role and learn from personal and organizational experience as means to ameliorate and gain professional excellence within the public service. Unlike political positions, public service positions are the backbone of an entire administration and are responsible for the stability of the public decision-making process and the democratic system as a whole. In that sense, the ability to "smell" and retain past policies while nurturing the ability to identify and adopt new and improved public measures is no less than critical in order to maintain the ability to govern and keep the democratic values in place.

The History and Science of Smell

Historical and cultural studies' focus on olfactory sense-making includes the way olfaction traverses social, cultural, and moral order. The sense of smell is formally defined as an act (verb), that is, how people manage smell while odor is conceived as a condition (noun). Olfactory sense-making can be defined as the process by which social and cultural meanings mediate between the act of smelling and the condition of odor. (Halton 2004) Thus, the process of attribution of meaning to odors can be traced from antiquity to modern times.

The sense of smell plays a prominent role in religious rituals, and olfactory imagery and metaphoric elements in many religious texts. In the Bible, we see examples of the use of the sense of smell, Myrrh and Frankincense (Olibanum, the biblical Levona), for example, served in religious ceremonies in the Holy Temple and for healing purposes. In ancient Egypt, Egyptian priests blended exotic scents to use in daily religious ceremonies to create a sensory experience for the temples' visitors and prayers. The historical and cultural studies of South Asian religions emphasize the role of the sense of smell in Hindu, Jain, and Buddhist religious rituals.

During the late Middle Ages, the scent of the air first stimulated debate over waste disposal with the advent of harmful disease-carrying odors. (Jørgensen 2013) Certain odors were interrelated with cultural conceptions of both disease and disgust. Besides waste thrown into rivers, street gutters were filled with trash that caused putrefying smells. In 1393, King Richard II ordered the local authorities to clean the gutters. (Jørgensen 2008) The smell of organic wastes pushed medieval governments to develop sanitary practices such as waste disposal sites located far from the populated areas and using soil to cover wastes. (Woolgar 2006)

In a way, the sense of smell as a subject for historical and cultural research became important in order to understand historical change and cultural categories through the way people projected their fears, desires, and prejudices onto smells. By the nineteenth century, the power of smell was reflected in shaping social practices and demarcating social hierarchies and spaces between "the deodorized bourgeoisie" and "the foul-smelling masses" as well as between commodity markets in the Western and non-Western worlds. (Classen, Howes, and Synnott 1994)

The biological mechanism by which we perceive scents is quite complex. The sense of smell is a very direct sense. The process of smelling is mediated by specialized sensory cells of the nasal cavity of vertebrates, so there is no transformation of the scent on its way to the brain. The chemicals that activate the olfactory process are called odorants. Each of the hundreds of odorant receptors is encoded by a different gene and each recognizes different odorants. Each scent is composed of several scent molecules, which is analogous to how words are built of letters. The process of olfactory coding, that is, how olfactory information is coded in the brain leading to certain perception, is still being studied and it is not yet entirely understood. When an odorant is detected by receptors, the olfactory receptor cells locate the odorant and then the brain reintegrates the odorant for identification and perception of the scent. (Auffarth 2013)

The sense of smell is linked to the part of the brain that affects our emotions. Researchers from various scientific disciplines such as psychology, biology, anatomy, and recently marketing, show that the physical and neural proximity of the olfactory system is associated with emotional memory. (Engen and Ross 1973; Herz 1997; Krishna 2010) Human beings are able to distinguish and remember more than 10,000 different scents. (Buck and Axel 1991) For example, Deethardt's (2002) research examined participants' ability to remember paired word associations where words were matched with specific aromas from seven combinations of dry teas, spices, and incense. Ludvigson and Rottman's (1989) study tested the capacities of participants in completing analogies, math problems, and vocabulary recall while being exposed to scents of cloves and lavender. Studies have demonstrated the capacity of humans to distinguish among different scents and to identify scents they were previously exposed to even after long periods of time. (Schab and Crowder 1995)

A relatively recent and increasing use of the sense of smell is for marketing purposes. In consumer behavior studies, the sense of smell is suggested to hold almost 50 percent of the consumer's communication with a firm's brand. (Gobe 2001) Shops that use conditioning smells that significantly impact consumers' behaviors tend to be better assessed by the consumers. (Chebat and Michon 2003) Good smell is effective in creating consumers' positive perceptions of product quality and environment. (Krishna, Lwin, and Morrin 2010) For example, Abercrombie and Fitch intentionally designs its retail stores based on sensory experience by developing its own line of men's fragrances called "Fierce", which is sprayed in stores in healthy doses to facilitate the firm's brand awareness and establish a sustainable brand image of a "lifestyle . . . packed with confidence and a bold, masculine attitude".

The use of smell as a positive sensory experience effect for hospital patients is illustrated in the case of Florida Hospital's Seaside Imaging Center. Due to the large number of cancellations among patients facing an MRI, the hospital addressed the problem by using ScentAir machines to diffuse the fragrance of vanilla in the MRI room, since the scent reportedly creates a pleasant environment that helps people feel less claustrophobic. (Hultén, Broweus, and van Dijk 2009, 62)

In the context of public organizations, smell triggers personal and institutional memory and provides a broader perspective over time, which then becomes effective in justifying the added values of public administration professionals. When first smelling a new scent, one always links it to an event, a person, a thing, or even a moment in time. Olfaction is thus an emotionally tied capability. (Herz and Engen 1996)

The perception of scents is of great importance in considering an appropriate sensorial strategy to enhance communication (e.g., communicating the public service values and professional identity). Since the complexity of the public service environment and its changes overload the public servant's learning capacity, ethics management becomes more dependent on communication, collective perception, and interpretation of values and codes of ethics. This, in turn, is often dependent on private memories and organizational long-term professional knowledge.

In the following section, the sense of smell is utilized as an ethics management strategy. To put the idea of smell as sensory experience into a practical setting in managing ethics in the public service, we discuss some strategies for retaining memory capabilities of public servants, which they use to support organizational action. We believe that since human memory is not well understood, the use of smell as a sensory strategy, although somewhat vague, will provide insights into the daily practices problems of public servants, as well as show how managers and technological advances can cooperate to elucidate these problems.

Smell as a Sensorial Strategy for Ethics Management in the Public Service

According to Gadamer (1997, 302), one's perception of a given situation can be referred to as a "Horizon". This definition does not limit the person's standpoint merely to what can be seen in the situation, rather it also allows the individual to see beyond. However, one person's horizon can and should be distinguished from another's, taking into account one's history, culture, past experiences, and many other prejudices or pre-judgments. When becoming acquainted with new situations, Gadamer estimates that our inherent prejudices are obliged to face a new and unknown reality and a "Fusion of Horizons" occurs. This describes the positive clash between inherent, sometimes outdated concepts and new ones changing one's perception.

It is only through this fusion of horizons that progress can be made. It is through this process of interpretation of the new and re-evaluation of the old, that "we participate in the production of a richer, more encompassing context of meaning and gain a more profound understanding not only of the other but also of ourselves". (Ramberg and Gjesdal 2014) This hermeneutic perspective allows the individual, immersed in his or her own biases, to explore new perspectives and broaden their horizons.

This directly and inversely relates to the somatic interpretation of the sense of smell, which draws back on personal memories. It has been proved that smell triggers personal memories to an earlier period of time and in a stronger manner than any other sensory experience. (Willander and Larsson 2006) It can thus be paralleled to a hermeneutic experience; immersed with personal biases and life-time experiences, the individual acknowledges a familiar smell and is drawn back to an early moment in time. This creates a new experience when the "old" instant connotation is now interpreted in a new manner, based on personal bias and life-time experiences, leading to the creation of a "fusion of horizons". Thus, the sense of smell can be viewed as a facilitator of continuity of values and the formation of new ones, while serving as a learning tool.

This interpretation of the olfactory sensory experience can be paralleled to institutional memory. Organizational memory is defined as the "information and knowledge known by the organization and the processes by which such information is acquired, stored and retrieved by organization members". (Anand, Manz, and Glick 1998, 796) However, the concept of organizational memory may provide more than just metaphor, but rather an analytical strategy to denote specific cognitive capacities for sharing and distributing knowledge at the organizational level. As suggested by Moorman and Miner (1998, 708):

> As an example of the content and level of memory, an organization that has been working in a particular industry for an extended period of time will likely accumulate a high level of declarative memory about the competitive structure and detailed traits of this industry. It might also accumulate a number of standard practices for dealing with others in the industry, representing a high level of procedural memory.

Following Moorman and Miner's definition, the use of organizational memory is helpful in understanding decision-making processes in which organizations are viewed as person-like entities. (Walsh and Ungson 1991) A basic assumption in the study of organizations is that organizations exhibit memory that is similar in function to the memory of individuals. (Daft and Weick 1984) The information received by the organization is processed and can be later retrieved from the organizational memory.

We would therefore argue that organizational memory can be utilized to promote ethical conduct within the public service. It is the public sector's moral duty to retain and learn from previous experience, while at the same time evolve and advance with the goal of providing better public service. Ongoing institutional learning with the aim of reaching new horizons is not less than an ethical obligation and a moral commitment of the public institution to the public it serves in a democratic society. In terms of public service, it seems only natural, then, to suggest that lack of familiarization with past policies, regulations, and even tacit know-how, would create an atmosphere of uncertainty, would compromise the quality of any public service, and would go against the basic raison d'être of the public service.

The public interest is naturally advanced when public administrators use their ability to retain past experiences and apply it for future reference in favor of the public. The "smell" of a successful or unsuccessful public endeavor is highly important for a public servant, especially in accessing previous knowledge, which makes it possible to re-apply proven solutions or best practices and to avoid past mistakes. In what follows we introduce several practical methods for this purpose.

Maintaining institutional memory within the public service allows the administrators to follow the strategy inherent in the development of olfactory sensory experience. One of the most common uses of institutional memory is the ability to create precedents. This implies the professional obligation to apply similar solutions to similar circumstances. In the legal field, precedents are considered essential in order to secure the necessary uniformity of the law and to strengthen the predictability of decisions. (Schreuer and Weiniger 2008) The same does not only apply in the public service, but is even enhanced. The application of identical solutions to identical problems strengthens the notion of justice and equality to all. The culture and the structure of the organization that promotes the practice of learning from past experience include the values of transparency, integrity, and accountability, which are extremely relevant and critical in the public service. (Lipshitz, Popper, and Friedman 2002)

The integrity of public servants and of the public institution as a whole, together with the faculty of the public to access information and the decision-making process, while holding the public agents accountable for their decisions and acts, represent an ethical and moral obligation. From the public sector's point of view, allowing full access to the administrative decision-making process obliges the administrators to be held accountable for their acts and calls for a high level of professionalism. From the citizens' point of view, integrity, transparency, and accountability would generate a greater trust in the public mechanisms and would eventually become a facilitator for greater citizen participation in the public sphere. (Armstrong 2005) Allowing the public to be part of the public process enables better understanding of policies in place, diminishes uncertainties, and creates a sense of confidence towards the public service.

While the administration should allow public information to be transparent and as accessible as possible, it is also the citizen's responsibility to remain active and promote policies and regulations affecting them. Active citizenship enables both the administrators and the citizens to better communicate and promote critical engagement with each other. Moreover, active citizenship is believed to be associated with effective political institutions, political and administrative decision-making, and the performance of public organizations as a whole. (Putnam 1993; Tam 1998) Thus, basing citizen engagement on institutional memory allows both sides to learn from past experience, analyze previous policy implementation, learn the needs and limitations of both sides, and promote a constant and critical dialogue.

Within the public administration, it is important to note, however, that organizational memory is not solely owned by the most senior and experienced of public servants. The public organization's ability to maintain quality public service for the long-term would be conditioned by its ability to constantly evolve and adapt itself to changing times and changing needs. Learning from past experience is indeed critical, while maintaining the ability to sense and identify winds of change and respond accordingly.

Knowledge sharing is a key component in the public organization's ability to preserve and utilize its organizational memory. Since interpretation of issues, problems, and solutions is an individual activity, it is through the sharing of information, knowledge, and tacit know-hows that the organizational interpretation system transcends the individual level. (Weick and Gilfillan 1971) This would allow the organization to learn from past experiences and share lessons learned with others, thus allowing potential new methods and mechanisms to emerge within the organization.

Public servants' education is highly important as well for the organization's ability to provide quality public service. This is especially true in light of the dynamic nature of the public service, constantly dependent on societal, political, technological, and structural variables. It is thus suggested that public services hold a dual educational mechanism; on the one hand, internal knowledge being transmitted from the most senior to the most junior, and on the other hand, periodic renewal and refinement of existing policies in light of the changing reality and emerging new needs.

Similar to the way familiar smells automatically draw the individual back to a certain moment in time (Reid et al. 2015), familiar incidents in the public service should draw the administrators back to their personal or institutional memory. Referring to precedents and applying them in the public decision-making process is the ethical responsibility of the public service.

However, reference made to institutional memory within the public service does not limit public servants to maintaining old habits alone. This fusion of horizons between a new given situation and past experiences calls for public servants to not only "steer", but to do so in new and innovative directions, rather than follow previous paths without proper reflection. In practice, when dealing with a new situation drawing on familiar traits, the public servant should indeed refer back to previous solutions, while analyzing and considering their relevance to the current given situation and, if needed, adapting and applying new solutions. While institutional memory is a key element in the public sphere, it does not limit public institutions to automatically applying old solutions to new problems. Quite the contrary—it calls for constant evolution, identification of new public needs, and the initiation of new public services. Valuable learning from past experience, organizational knowledge, and evaluation can be enhanced by using storytelling technique. (Gabriel 2000) The importance of the storytelling mechanism lies in the hermeneutic approach of narrative sense-making that "affects what we see and even the logic we use to structure our thought". (Thatchenkery 2001, 115) The adoption of storytelling and narratives invites the members of the organization to engage with meaning for socializing and sharing experiences of past actions and norms of conduct. Narratives are regarded as symbolic forms of discourse that are a "framework for reality construction in the organization" (Brown 1986, 80), through which past experience is reflexively reconstituted, made meaningful, and made communicable to members of the organization.

It is thus suggested that public organizations adopt the "storytelling" strategy as a means to transfer valuable and sometimes critical information from the older generation to the younger one. This would facilitate the generation of understanding of public servants to put their own personal and institutional memory to use. By opting for this strategy, the younger generation can be immersed in an experiential manner into the culture of the public service and the vast experience it beholds.

It is also, however, important that the storytelling strategy would be adopted by the younger generation itself and shared with the senior public servants as means of rejuvenating the system and allowing new and updated mechanisms to be adopted and used. As described, the public service cannot afford to manifest stagnation in the face of changing times and the changing role of the State. In accordance with this changing role, the public service must be able to change as well, and adapt its services and its accessibility to the public. This can be achieved by allowing the integration of a new generation to the public service, tasked with obeying the institutional memory while remaining open and attentive to the changing needs of the public. New methods or rising needs would be shared with the senior generation and adapted by them as well, leading to unified working strategies providing consistent service.

Avoiding stagnation is critical for a quality public service. Much like in the private sector, the public sector must evolve with time and act dynamically in order to remain relevant and provide the public with the most adequate and required services. What some may call "Dynamic Governance" (Neo and Chen 2007) signifies that lack of learning capacity and innovation would inevitably lead to stagnation and decay in the face of the unpredictable, ever-changing global environment. Promoting the fusion of institutional and personal memory with openness to new methods when required may allow the public sector to provide the best possible service while remaining relevant and beneficial.

Institutional memory is also a crucial element in the formation of reforms. It allows any person or organization to make a truly needed change in the most adequate manner, while avoiding past mistakes and learning forward. It is important to note this is not merely the task of public servants alone, but of all those affected by the public service, thus the public as a whole. Indeed, these are the political decision-makers who make the rules; however, the administrators implementing it and the public impacted by it are no less important in shaping the reality of the rule. The uniqueness of an ethical and democratically sensitive public administration is in its ability to sense the need for change and be willing to adapt accordingly. This is the sense of a true public service, aimed at serving the public good in a democratic society.

In relation to the memory systems, knowledge is often examined from a perspective of its tacitness/explicitness. (Wilson, Goodman, and Cronin 2007) Explicit knowledge can be simply expressed and thus codified, while the tacit one—which derives from intuitive nature—is hard to formulate and formalize. (Argote and Ingram 2000; Gourlay 2006) Professional and institutional memory are in line with this tacit knowledge, which usually relies on the individuals composing the organizational corps. The ability of the organization to sustain itself and move forward is then conditioned and dependent upon those comprising it, thus lacking the ability to exist independently.

It is through the process of codification that tacit knowledge can become explicit. Such codification of tacit knowledge can be achieved by institutional memory preservation in the forms of recording, documenting, and mentoring. Knowledge transformation within the organizations, from and to all institutional levels, will allow the organization to have long-term sustainability. This would enable public sector organizations to apply knowledge from a situational and local context to other situations and by other parts of the organization. (Argote and Ingram 2000; Gourlay 2006) In this way, organizational memory refers to the way members of public organizations interpret all incoming knowledge and it prescribes certain behaviors within organization. (Moorman and Miner 1997)

Public administrators must adhere to the collective institutional memory, learning from past occasions and not allowing inequalities to repeat themselves. An ethical organization nurtures a culture of ethical behavior and relies heavily on years of experience, procedures of data collection, and practical know how. This creates an ethical work environment allowing zero-tolerance for ethical infringement. This mechanism is expected to strengthen the ethical culture of the organization and its professional identity. Public administrators should be empowered to share their experiences and learn from their peers with regard to professional behavior in general and in ethical decision-making processes in particular, in order to improve the quality of the public service delivered.

Bibliography

Anand, Vikas, Charles C. Manz, and William H. Glick. 1998. "An Organizational Memory Approach to Information Management." *Academy of Management Review* 23:796–810.

Argote, Linda, and Paul Ingram. 2000. "Knowledge Transfer: A Basis for Competitive Advantage in Firms." *Organizational Behaviour and Human Decision Processes* 82:150–69.

Armstrong, Elia. 2005. "Integrity, Transparency and Accountability in Public Administration: Recent Trends, Regional and International Developments and Emerging Issues." *United Nations, Department of Economic and Social Affairs*, 1–10.

Auffarth, Benjamin. 2013. "Understanding Smell—The Olfactory Stimulus Problem." *Neuroscience & Biobehavioral Reviews* 37:1667–79.

Brown, M. H. 1986. "Sense Making and Narrative Forms: Reality Construction in Organizations." In *Organizational Communication: Emerging Perspectives I*, edited by Lee Thayer and George A. Barnett, 71–84. Norwood, NJ: Ablex.

Buck, Linda, and Richard Axel. 1991. "A Novel Multigene Family May Encode Odorant Receptors: A Molecular Basis for Odor Recognition." *Cell* 65:175–87.

Chebat, Jean-Charles, and Richard Michon. 2003. "Impact of Ambient Odors on Mall Shoppers' Emotions, Cognition, and Spending: A Test of Competitive Causal Theories." *Journal of Business Research* 56:529–39.

Classen, Constance, David Howes, and Anthony Synnott. 1994. *Aroma: The Cultural History of Smell*. New York: Routledge.

Daft, Richard L., and Karl E. Weick. 1984. "Toward a Model of Organizations as Interpretation Systems." *Academy of Management Review* 9:284–95.

Deethardt, Mark Richard. 2002. "The Effects of Olfactory Stimulation on Short-Term Memory." http://clearinghouse.mwsc.edu/manuscripts/347.asp (2003.06.12).

Engen, Trygg, and Bruce M. Ross. 1973. "Long-Term Memory of Odors with and without Verbal Descriptions." *Journal of Experimental Psychology* 100:221–7.

Gabriel, Yiannis. 2000. *Storytelling in Organizations, Facts, Fictions, and Fantasies*. Oxford, UK: Oxford University Press.

Gadamer, Hans-Georg. 1997. *Truth and Method*. New York: Continuum.

Gobe, Marc. 2001. *Emotional Branding: The New Paradigm for Connecting Brands to People*. New York: Allworth Press.

Gourlay, Stephen. 2006. "Conceptualizing Knowledge Creation: A Critique of Nonaka's Theory." *Journal of Management Studies* 43:1415–36.

Halton, Eugene. 2004. "The Living Gesture and the Signifying Moment." *Symbolic Interaction* 27:89–114.

Herz, Rachel S. 1997. "The Effects of Cue Distinctiveness on Odor-Based Context Dependent Memory." *Memory & Cognition* 25:375–80.

———, and Trygg Engen. 1996. "Odor Memory: Review and Analysis." *Psychonomic Bulletin & Review* 3:300–13.

Hultén, Bertil, Niklas Broweus, and Maracus van Dijk. 2009. *Sensory Marketing*. Basingstoke: Palgrave Macmillan.

Jørgensen, Dolly. 2008. "Cooperative Sanitation: Managing Streets and Gutters in Late Medieval England and Scandinavia." *Technology and Culture* 49:547–67.

———. 2013. "The Medieval Sense of Smell, Stench and Sanitation." In *Les cinq sens de la ville du Moyen Âge à nos jours*, edited by Ulrike Krampl, Robert Beck, and Emmanuelle Retaillaud-Bajac, 301–13. Tours: Presses Universitaires François-Rabelais.

Krishna, Aradhna. 2010. *Sensory Marketing: Research on the Sensuality of Products*. New York: Routledge.

———, May O. Lwin, and Maureen Morrin. 2010. "Product Scent and Memory." *Journal of Consumer Research* 37:57–67.

Lipshitz, Raanan, Micha Popper, and Victor Friedman. 2002. "A Multi-Facet Model of Organizational Learning." *Journal of Applied Behavioral Science* 38:78–98.

Ludvigson, H. Wayne, and Theresa R. Rottman. 1989. "Effects of Ambient Odors of Lavender and Cloves on Cognition, Memory, Affect and Mood." *Chemical Senses* 14:525–36.

Moorman, Christine, and Anne S. Miner. 1997. "The Impact of Organizational Memory on New Product Performance and Creativity." *Journal of Marketing Research* 34:91–106.

———. 1998. "Organizational Improvisation and Organizational Memory." *The Academy of Management Review* 23:698–723.

Neo, Boon Siong, and Geraldine Chen. 2007. "Dynamic Governance: Embedding Culture, Capabilities and Change in Singapore." *Capabilities and Change in Singapore*, July 3, 2007. http://dx.doi.org/10.2139/ssrn.1477817

Putnam, Robert D. 1993. *Making Democracy Work: Civic Traditions in Modern Italy*. Princeton, NJ: Princeton University Press.

Ramberg, Bjørn, and Kristin Gjesdal. 2014. "Hermeneutics." In *The Stanford Encyclopedia of Philosophy*, edited by Edward N. Zalta. http://plato.stanford.edu/archives/win2014/entries/hermeneutic

Reid, Chelsea A., Jeffrey D. Green, Tim Wildschut, and Constantine Sedikides. 2015. "Scent-Evoked Nostalgia." *Memory* 23:157–66.

Schab, Frank R., and Robert G. Crowder. 1995. "Implicit Measures of Odor Memory." In *Memory for Odors*, edited by Frank R. Schab and Robert G. Crowder, 72–91. Florence, KY: Psychology Press.

Schreuer, Christoph, and Matthew Weiniger. 2008. "A Doctrine of Precedent?" In *Oxford Handbook of International Investment Law*, edited by Peter Muchlinski, Federico Ortino, and Christoph Schreuer, 1188–206. Oxford, UK: Oxford University Press.

Tam, Henry. 1998. *Communitarianism: A New Agenda for Politics and Citizenship*. London: Macmillan.

Thatchenkery, Tojo Joseph. 2001. "Mining for Meaning: Reading Organizations Using Hermeneutic Philosophy." In *The Language of Organization*, edited by Robert Westwood and Stephen Linstead, 112–31. London: Sage.

Walsh, James P., and Gerardo Rivera Ungson. 1991. "Organizational Memory." *Academy of Management Review* 16:57–91.

Weick, Karl E., and David P. Gilfillan. 1971. "Fate of Arbitrary Traditions in Laboratory Microculture." *Journal of Personality and Social Psychology* 17:179–91.

Willander, Johan, and Maria Larsson. 2006. "Smell Your Way Back to Childhood: Autobiographical Odor Memory." *Psychonomic Bulletin & Review* 13:240–4.

Wilson, Jeanne M., Paul S. Goodman, and Matthew A. Cronin. 2007. "Group Learning." *Academy of Management Review* 32:1041–59.

Woolgar, C. M. 2006. *The Senses in Late Medieval England*. New Haven, CT: Yale University Press.

8   Touch

Touch implies an active engagement with someone or something. It is in this respect that we encourage public servants to act dynamically and engage with the public, while, in turn, encouraging the public to play an active role in the public sphere. By reaching out to the public, the administration implies that citizens ought not to be taken for granted and whose trust in the public administration must be acquired and constantly maintained. Active engagement with the public and the sharing of public decision-making processes and protocols will enhance the citizens' loyalty towards the administration and, in due course, also their trust.

The History and Science of Tactile

The sense of touch is an active explorative, informative, and complex somatosensory perceptual system. (Heller 2000; Klatzky, Lederman, and Reed 1987) Touch is gained through the somatic sensory system that has nerve receptors (also called tactile receptors) that feel pain, smoothness, roughness, and temperature changes such as hot and cold, and when something comes into direct contact with the skin. During the act of touching, receptors send signals in the cerebral cortex. The hormone oxytocin is produced when the touching experience is pleasant. Scheele et al. (2014) showed that oxytocin raises the levels of positive physiological response affected by interpersonal touch.

In 1931, Géza Revesz introduced the term "haptics". The term originated from the Greek words *haptikos*, meaning "able to touch", and *haptesthai*, which denotes "able to lay hold of". (Katz 1989; Révész 1950) Haptic perception has been delineated as "the assessment of products by touch through the hands, as important for the evaluation of product attributes that vary in terms of their texture, hardness, temperature, and weight". (Peck and Childers 2003a)

Haptics differs from other senses as it enables us to modify and manipulate the environment surrounding us. (McLaughlin, Hespanha, and Sukhatme 2002) The sense of touch develops in the womb and allows the embryo to gain information of its place in the womb. With the use of other senses such as hearing, seeing, smelling, or tasting we are unable to manipulate our environment; this is possible only through haptic body movements. In addition, the sense of touch can leave its mark on the body itself; for example, by exposing the skin to the sun, it can become dry and roughened by the wind. (Howes 2005, 33) According to Field (2001, 57), "Touch is ten times stronger than verbal or emotional contact, and it affects damned near everything we do. No other sense can arouse you like touch. We forget that touch is not only basic to our species, but the key to it." Thus, the sense of touch is said to be the most reliable sense, and is perceived as even more trustworthy than the sense of sight. (Sekuler and Blake 2002)

Touch sensory experience is a growing field of research especially in engineering, robotics, developmental and experimental psychology, cognitive science, and computer science since haptic interface devices are able to provide for simultaneous information exchange between a user and a machine. (Hayward et al. 2004) In recent years the sensory experience of touch has been widely used for technology appliances such as touch computer screens, touch TVs, and mobile phones. Touch detecting sensors incorporated into the monitor enable issuing commands to the computer by having it sense the position of the user's finger. Much like in human interaction, touch creates a more intimate sensation for the user, being able to operate the device with his or her bare hands rather than a button or a tele command. Moreover, digital technology produces touch experience through pressures and vibrations that provide the subjective feeling of presence to users. (Hulten 2013)

From a different perspective, some would find the sense of touch at risk in light of recent technological advancements. For instance, the sensation of writing a letter on a piece of paper has been overwhelmingly over-shadowed by virtual correspondence, as well as the notion of sensing a book or a newspaper which, while still existent, been undermined by e-books and news portals. In terms of human interaction, this, too, has been revolutionized with the increasing amount of virtual social activities, often times in place of physical contact and interaction. To respond to the prevailing demand of physical touch, various technological advancements also enable physically touching virtual objects represented within the computer, creating the illusion of interacting with solid physical objects. (Massie 1996)

The perceptual power of touch has also been demonstrated in studies on infant development and their interaction with the world around them, for example, whether they need a mother's touch or basic nutrition. Research conducted with infant macaque monkeys have found that the infant monkeys desired to remain closer to a surrogate cloth mother that provides warmth than the wire mother that provides nutrition. (Harlow 1958)

Similar preference for physical contact has been demonstrated in human infants, where acts of holding, cradling, or massaging the baby improved parent–infant attachment and the baby's emotional and physiological well-being. (Montagu 1986) It also seems the need for touch does not lessen over the years and is even enhanced in older age. While various senses may experience reduced functionality over the years, such as vision or hearing, the sense of touch is left intact. It is on those occasions that the sense of touch becomes a communication tool allowing the elderly to reach out and remain in contact with their environment. In this sense, touch enables a certain notion of control and presence, even when other senses begin to fail, slowly isolating the individual from his surroundings. (Vortherms 1991)

However, the question remains whether touch is a universal desire or whether everyone has the same need for touch. Peck and Childers (2003b) have created the Need-for-Touch scale, which collected individual differences in need-for-touch. The scale is constructed by two sub-scales—instrumental and autotelic. The instrumental need for touch denotes functionality, i.e., touching with a specific objective. The autotelic need for touch focuses on the emotional component of touch—the pleasant feeling of touching objects.

Despite apparent differences in desire for interpersonal touch, altogether studies have shown that physical touch improves team performance, such as in the case of NBA basketball players, by creating norms of cooperation. (Kraus, Huang, and Keltner 2010) Interpersonal touch is also assumed to enhance information flow and communication in clinical and professional settings. (Fisher, Rytting, and Heslin 1976)

In short, humans have an important social and personal need to use touch as an effective communication channel for conveying intimacy that builds strong emotional bonds. However, despite the social richness of touch and its key role in human social interaction, existing public service practices still rely on sound and vision and do not use haptic interaction to create collaborative environments and positive forms of interaction. In the following section, we offer to show how inclusionary practices can be considered demonstrations of the potential devices and applications of social touch in the public service.

Touch as a Sensorial Strategy for Ethics Management in the Public Service

For the purpose of this book, we would like to offer a broader perspective to the sense of touch, considering outreach activities and inclusionary practices as a form of touching the public. Western bureaucratic public systems are oftentimes distinct from the public itself, creating alienation between the public and the institutionalized public entities. This approach is rooted back in the Weberian tradition where a clear distinction should be drawn between the politics, the bureaucratic agencies, and the public itself, which has led to a culture of Top-Down politics, where only those in power dictate the rules and regulations by which society should be ruled. (Robinson 2015) This has resulted in a growing indifference in the public sphere and in a clear lack of trust on behalf of the public in the governmental institutions.

In recent years and with the introduction of the New Public Management theory and practices, more and more governments are seeking to regain the lost public trust and re-engage the public in the administrative decision-making process and implementation. After all, the main objective of the public administration is to fulfill the public interest, a task it can only accomplish through reaching out to the public and collecting information regarding its needs and preferences.

In the information era we live in it has become possible to remove all barriers leading to knowledge and information. It has also become viable to reach out to the public and consult them on policy issues through various technological means. E-government can most certainly play an important role in reaching out and "taking the public's pulse". E-government can be defined as "the use of Information and Communications Technologies and its application by the government for the provision of information and public services to the people". (United Nations 2004) E-government facilitates interaction with the public and allows participative decision-making for the benefit of the public. This way, by launching an interactive Internet campaign regarding construction plans in a certain area, for example, public agencies can collect a vast amount of information from the public which they might not otherwise have been aware of, allowing them to better adjust and design the actions of the public administration. Crowdsourcing is also a very effective and commonly used tool in the effort to reach out and in order to create a direct bond between the public and the administration, as well as offering a civil service better adjusted to the public.

These methods would somewhat bring us back to the era of the Greek Participatory Democracy, where the citizens played an active role in the formation of public policies and their implementation methods. Certainly, a lot has changed in terms of the participatory level of citizens in the public administration since then, going as far as the opposite direction where only a minority chooses to actively engage in public activities. However, it seems that e-government could offer an opportunity to regain some of the lost public participation, using tools familiar and accessible to the public. We would name it "Participatory Democracy 2.0", i.e., reaching out to the public in order to encourage the return of the public's engagement via new technological tools.

Public servants should also strive to actively reach out to professionals and decision-makers as well as conduct comparable analysis both locally and internationally, in order to gain the most accurate and comprehensive information possible. Placed in the middle between the public and the political instances, public servants will be able to operate in a close two-way circuit where information is constantly coming from the public and/or decision-makers and returns to the public and/or decision-makers after being revised, enhanced, and analyzed by both. It is therefore understood that the public administration is no longer the exclusive owner of information, which can be provided in a bottom-up manner just as much as in a top-down manner.

Other than reaching out to the public, the administration must sustain an inclusionary approach, inviting all parts of the population to participate in the public sphere in an equal manner. Inclusionary practices involve a clear recognition according to which individuals or groups are sometimes treated unfairly or excluded because of their differences. Other than reaching out to all equally, for effective inclusionary initiatives to be realized public administrators must also be viewed as legitimate conveners of public interaction in the name of legal compliance to earn the public's trust. This would enable them to operate not only as gatekeepers of legality, but also as proactive problem solvers who assist in constituting systems that advance equity within legal boundaries.

Inclusion refers to the act of being accepted and able to participate fully within the family, the community, and the society within which one lives. (Guildford 2000) People who are excluded, whether because of poverty, ill-health, gender, race, or ethnicity, do not have the opportunity to fully enjoy the social and economic benefits their community or society has to offer. Social inclusion denotes the need to accept someone into interpersonal interactions and social networks. Thus, considerable attention has been paid to defining social exclusion as the opposite of social inclusion.

Social exclusion was first coined in France in 1974 and since then has been recognized across disciplinary contexts ranging from academic and professional to political arenas. Social exclusion has been used to identify an underclass that fell outside the protection of the State's social insurance. These groups were labeled "mentally and physically handicapped, suicidal people, aged invalids, abused children, substance users, delinquents, single parents, multi-problem households, marginal asocial persons, and other social 'misfits'." (Silver 1995, 63)

Within political, academic, and professional discourses, social exclusion is often associated with terms such as poverty and scarcity, which confines it largely to the context of social and economic policy. However, the growing use of social exclusion, instead of poverty or deprivation, in the area of policy analysis and decision-making is due largely to the recognition that poverty has been seen as too narrow and limiting a concept in addressing the social problems. (Bhalla and Lapeyre 1997; Walker and Walker 1997) According to Room (1995), for example, poverty is defined in terms of re-allocation and re-distribution of resources, whereas social exclusion is concerned with relational issues (emphasizing the relations between an individual and various potential support networks such as family, friends, community, and State services and institutions).

The multidimensional feature inherent in the concept of social exclusion incorporates mainly economic, social, and political dimensions. Bhalla and Lapeyre (1997, 430) identify these three interrelated dimensions of social exclusion for "It is useful to demonstrate that political freedom and civil rights and liberties can draw the best out of people and raise their productivity, thereby contributing to growth and overcoming economic exclusion." The economic dimension is associated with income and production issues as well as access to goods and services: social exclusion thus results from "income and livelihood, and from the satisfaction of such basic needs as housing/shelter, health and education". (Bhalla and Lapeyre 1997, 418) The social dimension of social exclusion is concerned with social values such as self-identity, dignity, the role of community and other supportive networks that secure the level of social integration, and relational ties between individuals and society and individuals and the State. Following Bhalla and Lapeyre's conceptualization of social exclusion, the social dimension includes access to social services (e.g., health and education), access to the labor market, and the opportunity for social participation and its effects on social integration. The political dimension of exclusion includes access to various rights, such as civil (e.g., the right to justice, freedom of expression), political ("the right to participate in the exercise of political power"), and socioeconomic, and addresses matters of equality of opportunity, right to minimum welfare benefits, etc.

Increased efforts to involve citizens at all levels of government as a hallmark of good governance in democracies were aimed at empowering citizens to become active policy shapers who have a say in the decisions that affect their lives. As entrenched by the OECD report:

> Engaging citizens in policy making is a sound investment and a core element of good governance. It allows governments to tap wider sources of information, perspectives, and potential solutions, and improves the quality of the decisions reached. Equally important, it contributes to building public trust in government, raising the quality of democracy and strengthening civic capacity.
>
> (OECD 2001, 11)

However, effective participation left the question of inclusion unsolved. Studies have shown that citizen participation committees are usually composed of members of the top socioeconomic group. (Abel and Stephan 2000; Russell and Vidler 2000; Weber 2000) Thus, lower class citizens of low-income status have been faced with difficulties and barriers to participate since their priorities were always to provide basic needs for their families, which denied them time to spend engaging in public practices. E-government, as mentioned above, is also challenged by inclusive participation, as lower economic classes as well as elderly or handicapped people are denied the possibility to participate in the democratic process taking place through technological means.

Thus, effective inclusive citizen participation should advocate participation as a way to allow powerless or underrepresented groups to interact with other groups in society to gain legitimacy as political players, and participate in the deliberative process in order to tackle a range of policy issues. This may signify that in certain areas and/or with regard to certain populations, other means such as focus groups, meetings, and polls might be more effective in collecting information and translating it into change in the public administration. It is important that public agents know the population they aim to serve in order to pursue the best-suited outreach activities for them, not only encouraging them to participate in the public effort but also obtaining effective and valuable results.

Inclusionary practices include, for example, Open Performance Circles, initiated by public administrators to encourage the participation of citizens in the evaluation of administrative procedures and services and give administrators a platform from which they can identify problems, suggestions, and critiques. It is clear that none of this would be made possible if public administrators would not take the initiative to actively engage with the public and remove procedural barriers to the participation of all populations, with special emphasis on disadvantaged or vulnerable groups. These are most frequently excluded due to age, disabilities, geographic distance, or literacy. It is critical to increase the disadvantaged populations' trust in the public institutions and servants as a pre-condition for a collaborative relationship.

With a shared vision of what inclusive public service looks like in practice, public administrators can initiate the actual planning process of having excluded citizens have access to policy decision-making by using the following a set of key questions:

- Are you able to identify who is being excluded?
- Are you able to identify the sources of exclusion in a given policy or program?
- Can you assess the short- and the long-term implications of existing policies on social exclusion?
- What are the costs and benefits of exclusion?
- Are there any policy instruments to address the problem of social exclusion?
- How will the policy or program increase or reduce discrimination on the basis of gender, race, age, culture, or ethnicity?
- How will the policy or program allow sufficient personal resources to allow all community members to participate in policy decision-making?
- What kind of policy instruments should be added or barriers removed to participation in public gatherings and in other forms of social interaction?
- How can inclusionary practices be encouraged among public administrators and sustained within the public service?

The active engagement of the public administration, be it on the local or national levels, is a two-way stream. This means that no less than the public servants are expected to reach out to the public, the public itself is expected to cooperate with the public instances and lead the civil society towards a more active long-standing involvement in the public decision-making process. In order for this to be made possible, the public must restore its trust in governmental agencies. As trust is a complex and multifaceted concept, much like other things often taken for granted, it is best appreciated when it is gone. At the most basic level of the public administration as a service provider, "Once the trust relationship has broken down, public employees find it more difficult to perform their tasks." (Yates 1982, 124) It is clear from this statement that a lack of trust makes it more difficult for all parties involved to cooperate with each other. The public questions the quality of service it receives, thus avoiding it as much as possible or finding alternatives, while the public servants are faced with constant criticism and considered to be inefficient and sometimes even redundant.

One of the leading methods to increase trust in the public administration is transparency. Governmental agencies have realized that they are regarded in a negative manner by the public and therefore are encouraged to express transparency, inviting the public to have a closer look and at times even participate in the administrative decision-making process. Transparent public agencies might be more frequently exposed to criticism; however, they are also very much appreciated for their willingness to make an effort in order to regain trust. A public institution that manages to regain the public trust increases its legitimacy in their eyes and is therefore seldom questioned. Such an institution will enjoy a high level of public participation and will, in turn, be able to provide the public with the best suited and appropriate public service. This ability to obtain the public trust is a critical step on the way to "touching" the public, since no engagement would be made possible as long as the public does not trust the organization or sees it as illegitimate.

Another important condition in order to engage with the public and create a meaningful interaction between the public and the government institutions is Accountability. The public service must be able to report its actions and remain responsible for them, be it under formal audits and control or in the bare eye of the public. According to Paul (1992, 1047), "Public accountability refers to the spectrum of approaches, mechanisms and practices used by the stakeholders concerned with public services to ensure a desired level and type of performance." Apart from the formal control mechanisms, the public can and should also play an important role in demanding and maintaining accountability in the public service. A responsible and accountable public service will once again gain the trust of the public and will facilitate any interaction between the institutions and the public itself.

Both transparency and accountability, facilitated by e-governments' mechanisms and inclusionary practices, make it easier and more natural for the public to put their trust in the hands of the public administration. Similar to human interaction, it is only when there is trust that a meaningful relationship can be formed and therefore only by achieving trust could the administration and the public come closer together. Using the sensory metaphor of touch, these mechanisms allow the public administration to reach out to the public and touch it, take its pulse, and react accordingly.

Bibliography

Abel, Troy D., and Mark Stephan. 2000. "The Limits of Civic Environmentalism." *American Behavioral Scientist* 44.4:614–28.

Bhalla, Ajit, and Frédéric Lapeyre. 1997. "Social Exclusion: Towards an Analytical and Operational Framework." *Development and Change* 28.3:413–33.

Field, Tiffany. 2001. *Touch*. Cambridge, MA: MIT Press.

Fisher, Jeffrey D., Marvin Rytting, and Richard Heslin. 1976. "Hands Touching Hands: Affective and Evaluative Effects of an Interpersonal Touch." *Sociometry* 39:416–21.

Guildford, Janet. 2000. *Making the Case for Social and Economic Inclusion*. Halifax, Nova Scotia: Population and Public Health Branch, Atlantic Regional Office, Health Canada.

Harlow, Harry F. 1958. "The Nature of Love." *American Psychologist* 13.12:673–85.

Hayward, Vincent, Oliver R. Astley, Manuel Cruz-Hernandez, Danny Grant, and Gabriel Robles-De-La-Torre. 2004. "Haptic Interfaces and Devices." *Sensor Review* 24:16–29.

Heller, Morton A. 2000. *Touch, Representation, and Blindness: Debates in Psychology*. Oxford, UK: Oxford University Press.

Howes, David. 2005. "Skinscapes." In *The Book of Touch*, edited by Constance Classen, 27–40. Oxford, UK: Berg Publishers.

Hulten, Bértil. 2013. "Sensory Cues as In-Store Innovations: Their Impact on Shopper Approaches and Touch Behavior." *Journal of Innovation Management* 1.1:17–37.

Katz, David. 1989. *The World of Touch*. Translated by Lester E. Krueger. Hillsdale, NJ: Lawrence Erlbaum.

Klatzky, Roberta L., Susan J. Lederman, and Catherine Reed. 1987. "There's More to Touch Than Meets the Eye: The Salience of Object Attributes for Haptics with and without Vision." *Journal of Experimental Psychology: General* 116:356–69.

Kraus, Michael W., Cassey Huang, and Dacher Keltner. 2010. "Tactile Communication, Cooperation, and Performance: An Ethological Study of the NBA." *Emotion* 10:745–9.

Massie, Thomas H. 1996. "Initial Haptic Explorations with the Phantom: Virtual Touch through Point Interaction." PhD dissertation, Massachusetts Institute of Technology, Department of Mechanical Engineering.

McLaughlin, Margaret L., João Pedro Hespanha, and Gaurav S. Sukhatme. 2002. *Touch in Virtual Environments*. New York: Prentice Hall.

Montagu, Ashley. 1986. *Touching*. New York: Harper Collins.

OECD. 2001. "Engaging Citizens in Policy Making: Information, Consultation and Public Participation." http://www.oecd.org/dataoecd/24/34/2384040.pdf

Paul, Samuel. 1992. "Accountability in Public Services: Exit, Voice and Control." *World Development* 20.7:1047–60.

Peck, Joann, and Terry L. Childers. 2003a. "To Have and to Hold: The Influence of Haptic Information on Product Judgments." *Journal of Marketing* 67.2:35–48.

———. 2003b. "Individual Differences in Haptic Information Processing: The 'Need for Touch' Scale." *The Journal of Consumer Research* 30.3:430–42.

Révész, Géza. 1950. *Psychology and Art of the Blind*. London: Green Longmans.

Robinson, Mark. 2015. *From Old Public Administration to the New Public Service Implications for Public Sector Reform in Developing Countries*. Singapore: United Nations Development Programme, Global Centre for Public Service Excellence.

Room, Graham. 1995. *Beyond the Threshold: The Measurement and Analysis of Social Exclusion*. Bristol, UK: Policy Press.

Russell, Steven, and Elizabeth Vidler. 2000. "The Rise and Fall of Government-Community Partnerships for Urban Development: Grassroots Testimony from Colombo." *Environment & Urbanization* 12.1:73–86.

Scheele, Dirk, Keith M. Kendrick, Christoph Khouri, Elisa Kretzer, Thomas E. Schläpfer, Birgit Stoffel-Wagner, Onur Güntürkün, Wolfgang Maier, and René Hurlemann. 2014. "An Oxytocin-Induced Facilitation of Neural and Emotional Responses to Social Touch Correlates Inversely with Autism Traits." *Neuropsychopharmacology* 39:2078–85.

Silver, Hilary. 1995. "Reconceptualizing Social Disadvantage: Three Paradigms of Social Exclusion." In *Social Exclusion, Rhetoric, Reality, Responses*, edited by Gerry Rodgers, Charles G. Gore, and José B. Figuerido, 58–80. New York: International Institute for Labor Studies/UNDP.

United Nations. 2004. "Global E-Government Readiness Report." https://public administration.un.org/egovkb/portals/egovkb/Documents/un/2004-Survey/Complete-Survey.pdf

Vortherms, Ruth C. 1991. "Clinically Improving COMMUNICATION through Touch." *Journal of Gerontological Nursing* 17.5:6–9.

Walker, Alan, and Carol Walker, eds. 1997. *Britain Divided: The Growth of Social Exclusion in the 1980s and 1990s*. London: Child Poverty Action Group Ltd.

Weber, Edward P. 2000. "A New Vanguard for the Environment: Grass-Roots Ecosystem Management as a New Environmental Movement." *Society & Natural Resources* 13.3:237–59.

Yates, Douglas. 1982. *Bureaucratic Democracy: The Search for Democracy and Efficiency in American Government*. Cambridge, MA: Harvard University Press.

9 Taste

Public servants, as representatives of the public interest in a democratic system, are tasked with acting tastefully, thus applying their sense of discretionary judgment and making sensible decisions. Professional public servants have the added importance of serving the public while playing a role in the central administration. It is therefore their role, within the limit of their authority and when necessary, to bridge these two worlds sensibly and tastefully.

The History and Science of Taste

The sense of taste, much like the sense of smell, is a chemical sense. There are five tastes including sweet, salty, sour, bitter, and umami. The last taste, umami, was discovered by Japanese scholars and is associated with the meaning of "savory, that obtained from monosodium glutamate (MSG) or the taste of pure protein". (Ikeda 2002) Humans sense taste with taste receptor cells. These cells are clustered in taste buds located on the tongue, although there are taste buds in the throat as well. A newborn child has taste buds on the inside of his cheek and his future taste preferences are influenced in the womb. (Romantshik et al. 2007; Varendi, Porter, and Winberg 2002)

The sensory experience of taste mediates relationships to the material world defined by corporeality and ephemerality. Due to these conditions, the sense of taste is regarded as the weakest sense; much of the taste experience incorporates smell and touch, placing it well below the much less dominant sensual faculties of sight and hearing. The dependence of the sense of taste on those senses has been demonstrated in various studies showing how the sense of smell (how the food smells) makes taste possible, touch intensifies taste textures (appropriate temperature, fattiness), and sight (how the food looks or is presented on a plate) and even hearing are part of the taste experience (the sound of crack when you bite). (Harvey 2011; Herz 2007; Jenner 2011) For example, a cook using sensory experience knows how much seeing and hearing audible crunchiness of certain foods (e.g., celery, breakfast cereals, popcorn, apples) has to do with what and how we taste. In the field of advertising, Elder and Krishna (2010) show that an ad incorporating multiple sensations (e.g., taste, touch, and smell) leads to better taste perception than one emphasizing taste unaided. In addition, the knowledge of ingredients affects taste perceptions when revealed before consumption. (Lee, Frederick, and Ariely 2006; Wansink et al. 2000)

In ancient Greece, Aristotle was one of the first to develop a list of basic tastes in which the two most basic tastes were sweet and bitter. (Polansky 2007) In ancient Indian healing science the list of basic tastes includes sweet, salty, sour, pungent, bitter, and astringent. (Trubek 2008) During the sixteenth century, wine and wheat emphasized the connection between taste and place. The taste experience of wine, for example, derived from the soil in which the grapes were grown. (Trubek 2008) The sense of taste was redefined during the eighteen century in terms of reason and refinement. The sense of taste became associated with spiritual characteristics and therefore as a quality that sets the individual apart. Edmund Burke demonstrates the influence of intellectualism and aestheticism movements on the sense of taste: "I mean by the word Taste no more than that faculty or those faculties of the mind, which are affected with, or which form a judgment of, the works of imagination and the elegant arts." (Burke 1767, 6; Gigante 2005a)

Since the nineteenth century, professionalism in the culinary field has concentrated on articulating values and applying scientific tools to overcome the problems of production of taste to satisfy elite consumers. (Gigante 2005b) Gastronomy, that is, the laws that govern the stomach, became an instrument of aesthetic sensitivity and intellectual judgment to legitimize a hierarchical social order. (Gigante 2005b) According to Brillat-Savarin, who published the book *The Physiology of Taste*, "Gastronomy is the knowledge and understanding of all that relates to man as he eats. Its purpose is to ensure the conservation of men, using the best food possible." (Montagné 1988) This modern conceptualization of taste incorporated the characteristic of "good taste" to demarcate the superiority of certain groups of cultural consumers endowed with intellectual capacities to develop preference for a given cultural product. (Gans 1999)

Brands apply taste in marketing management practices. (Krishna and Schwarz 2014) For example, Coca-Cola is one of the brands that identifies itself with the taste experience. (Nair 2013) For example, in its 2001 slogan in the United States, Canada, and the UK, the company opted for "Life tastes good", thus referring to their product as being equivalently as good as the act of living life itself. Marketing professionals in the restaurant industry use this strategic tool to increase restaurant sales. (Wansink, Ittersum, and Painter 2004) Recent studies of taste sensory marketing demonstrated that such strategy not only attracts the customers but also aims at increasing their loyalty. (Freitas da-Costa et al. 2012)

A gustatory taste is an evaluation of the flavor of foods that we immediately sense when food or other substance is placed on the tongue. It is a taste sensory experience that happens. However, this taste experience does not involve any decision or deliberation. We do not decide whether the piece of cheese pleases us or not. We are rather saying that what comes after is a review of the act of taste in light of that experience and past experience. It is within social, cultural, historical contexts that the taste in question is evaluated as good or bad.

Viewed in this way, taste making is the final referent and sanction of judgment. (Jessup 1960) Judgment is based on the capacity to compare and show taste in a meaningful stipulation to be different. The existence of differences validates differences in preferences or values. Taste making is considered as a collective interpretation of a symbol that results in a shared preference. (DiMaggio 1997) As Kant suggested, taste making is the province of universal, disinterested judgment based on responses of pleasure or displeasure which he describes as follows:

> When [a man] puts a thing on a pedestal and calls it beautiful, he demands the same delight from others. He judges not merely for himself, but for all men, and then speaks of beauty as if it were a property of things. Thus he says that the thing is beautiful; and it is not as if he counts on others agreeing with him in his judgment of liking owing to his having found them in such agreement on a number of occasions, but he demands this agreement of them. He blames them if they judge differently, and denies them taste, which he still requires of them as something they ought to have; and to this extent it is not open to men to say: Everyone has his own taste. This would be equivalent to saying that there is no such thing as taste, i.e. no aesthetic judgment capable of making a rightful claim upon the assent of all men.
>
> (Kant 1790/1928, 52; see also 136–9)

Although Kant does not address the nature of the "universality" or normativity that encompasses taste making, the pleasure one gets from a genuinely beautiful object does not lie in the fact that it is agreeable. Rather, the pleasure lies in how it makes him/her think. It stimulates deliberation of a particular kind that is a free play of understanding and imagination.

Contrary to Kant, a good taste besides being a sensory experience is an educated taste; it is informed, experienced, and developed. The acts of good taste are discriminating, extensive, tolerant, and integrated. Conversely, "bad taste" is associated with insensitivity due to impaired sense capacities or narrowness of mind or emotions, a taste that is badly informed, inexperienced, narrow, intolerant, provincial, and confused. For example, judgment of good taste unconsciously reflects discrimination in a negative sense, while the characteristic of tolerance is articulated in the way the evaluator does not respond immediately to stimuli of pleasure or displeasure in the presence of a food with which he is unfamiliar, of which he has no prior experience. The response towards the unfamiliar will in a way be a feeling of surprise and cautious interest.

When taste is the source of judgment on what is ethically good and evil, the question of respect comes under pressure. Respect, in this manner, is an evaluating concept that denotes a certain relation between a subject and an object. (Dilton 1995)

> A relationship between a subject and an object, in which the subject responds to the object from a certain perspective in some appropriate way. Respect necessarily has an object: respect is always for, directed toward, paid to, felt about, shown for some object. While a wide variety of things can be appropriate objects of one kind of respect or another, the subject of respect is always a person, that is, a conscious rational being capable of recognizing things, being self-consciously and intentionally responsive to them, and having and expressing values with regard to them. Though animals may love or fear us, only humans can respect and disrespect us or anything else.
>
> (Zalta 2006)

Public service professionals are both subjects and objects of respect. They are able to be familiar with and respond to objects of value. The objects of respect are those entrenched in ethics codes such as rights and obligations, the rightful faculty of doing and acting in a certain manner, versus the obligation to fulfill certain tasks and obey certain rules. Thus, the function of respect is very closely allied to the function of good taste; that is, conforming to a set of expectations or ideals of what is appropriate. For example, the American Society for Public Administration Code of Ethics makes much reference to respect; in article 1.e. it states: "Serve all persons with courtesy, respect, and dedication to high standards." Despite the fact that respect seems to be an all-encompassing value and frequently appears in professional norms and codes of ethics, what it requires in everyday contemporary public service practice is less than clear.

According to Raz (2001), there are two ways of relating to what is considered valuable and discerns between respecting it and engaging with it:

> We must respect what is valuable and it is wrong not to do so. We have reason to engage with what is valuable, and it is intelligible that we should do so. Sometimes it is foolish, rash, weak, defective in some other specific way, or even irrational to fail to engage with what is of greater value than available alternatives, or to engage with what is of lesser value. But it is not, generally speaking, wrong to do so.
>
> (Raz 2001, 6)

Raz actually draws three stages of correct reaction to value. First, there is the acknowledgment of value, by which Raz means that our emotions and thoughts should recognize the value of the object in question. The second stage concerns preservation and non-destruction. As explained by Raz (2001, 161):

> Respect for Michelangelo's work consists primarily in acknowledging his achievement in what we say, and think, and in caring for the preservation of the work. This fact reflects another: one need not be among those who spend time examining it and admiring it. Not everyone need be an art connoisseur, or a devotee of Michelangelo's work. But everyone ought to respect his work.

Raz also includes a third stage—engagement. Raz defines the practice of engagement in relation to respect by the way

> we do so when we listen to music with attention and discrimination, read a novel with understanding, climb rocks using our skill to cope, spend time with friends in ways appropriate to our relationships with them, and so on and so forth. The first two stages of relating to value contrast with the third. Ultimately, value is realised when it is engaged with. There is a sense in which music is there to be appreciated in listening and playing, novels to be read with understanding, friendships to be pursued, dances to be joined in, and so on. Merely thinking of valuable objects and preserving them is a mere preliminary to engaging with value . . . Yet, obviously no one has to engage with all valuable objects. We need not read all the novels, listen to all the music, climb all the mountains, go to all the parties, dance in all the dances, which are worthwhile.
>
> (2001, 262–3)

The significance of engagement as a component of respect needs to be active in paying close attention to service users, to become their advocates and intervene when they seem to have difficulty expressing their preferences or views on a given service. Although Raz's approach provides an insightful framework for the stages of appropriate responses to respect, what is needed is more clarity and guidance on applying respect in public service decision-making processes and daily practices. An account of respect that goes beyond engagement and advocacy must refer to human flourishing and moral capabilities that enable public servants to function out of refinement of taste. According to Haldane: "As a set of capacities for discerning value and an inclination for pursuing it taste is evidently a virtue and thus is worth cultivating." (1989, 20) We then aim to demonstrate how managers and public servants improve these capacities to discern excellence.

Our research aims to show that there is also another distinguishable function of the sense of taste that goes beyond the aim of sharpening the image of individuals or the aesthetic notion of collectives. The other aim is to evaluate, in which judgment is the defining characteristic. We would argue that the ability to apply judgment and make discretionary decisions relies on one's more or less developed sense of taste. It is the sense of taste that would affect the way one makes a decision or chooses between several options lying ahead. In other words, taste can be understood as a preference, a choice, and a stance being taken. Thus, having "good taste" would be interpreted as being able to make the right decision and choose the best option, while having "bad taste" would lead to unfavorable choices and unfortunate consequences for the sake of the individual, the group, or even the nation.

Taste can be used as a tool of evaluation to differentiate between good and bad taste. The logic behind the sense of taste is that the very nature of taste allows an analysis that helps to distinguish some tastes from others and to call some "good" and others "bad". Based on such a characteristic, it is possible to maintain a distinction that a judgment of taste is in fact a judgment. A judgment in terms of criteria or units of analysis selected as common ground to measure substances. The question remains then: What is considered good taste?

Taste as a Sensorial Strategy for Ethics Management in the Public Service

Taste in the public sphere and, more particularly, in the public service represents the tension between two ideas. The first would be the public servants' obligation to follow the administrative guidelines, and obey and implement the law, which serves as a framework for the public service. (Lewis and Gilman 2005) The purpose of these regulations is to uphold the general will and maintain the democratic nature of the State. The second idea, which may seem obvious yet requires emphasis, is the notion of service. The mere existence of public servants is dependent on their ability to satisfy the public's needs (Denhardt and Denhardt 2000) and to provide public goods that can only be provided by the State. According to Denhardt and Denhardt, the latter role is at times even more important than the first, and defines what makes the public service a service at all.

Public servants are tasked with managing the tension between these two competing yet complementary ideas, and we consider their ability to do so as relying on the extent to which they can properly apply their sense of taste. Clearly, this requires explanation. The sense of taste provides the public servants with a certain level of sensitiveness, allowing them to analyze and apply an ethical consideration of the situation at hand, with the aim to balance between the "public" and the "service".

Seen this way, acting tastefully signifies making value judgment calls and applying common sense. It follows the basic notion of distinguishing between "right" and "wrong" and practicing the inherent ability to make sensible decisions that lead to favorable outcomes. This process calls for a moral and ethical decision-making mechanism. Acting tastefully must entail making ethical considerations and opting for the moral alternative.

Taste is also a key concept of humanism (Anker 2012) as it entails the ability to act sensibly towards others, to show compassion, to know when it is appropriate to apply judgment, and when one should allow the individual to be. Taste as an intellectual capacity, far beyond the aesthetic or savory one, is the faculty to distinguish between good and bad, right and wrong, make the right judgment and apply it.

However, by which standards would "right" and "wrong" be defined? What would qualify a certain decision to be right, whereas a different one would be wrong? Clear answers to this could only be found in hindsight; however in real time when public servants are required to act or decide on a certain matter, their ability to make the tasteful and right choice would rely on the combination of their professionalism, personal character, and common sense.

Those three elements should be seen as one, since it is only when they are put together that a "right" decision can be made. One cannot make a correct judgment call without taking into consideration the professional customs and values appreciated in the specific field. Moreover, what one would consider to be right depends on its inherent ethical scale and values. To this we add common sense, common to all those in a particular society, which calls for the collective logic and appreciation of good and bad.

In these conditions, what would entail a tasteful behavior in the public administration? While laws and regulations within the public service must be upheld and applied equally to all, it seems unreasonable that all public servants would hold to the same standard of tasteful behavior. However, much like other components of the Code of Ethics, tasteful behavior can and must be apprehended. (Stevens 1999) A breakdown of the significance of "tasteful" public servants' behavior might be useful.

Acting tastefully can be interpreted as acting sensibly; hence, acting in a respectful manner to all. This requires both intelligence and sensibility. However, the public system, providing vast services to the entire public, must uphold equal standards to all and operate in an effective manner. Thus, according to Lipsky (1980), it often leads public agents to provide service in an automatic and even machine-like manner as a coping mechanism to deal with their work environment and workload. One solution to this might be technological, in accordance with the New Public Management paradigm (Hood 1991) and even more so the e-Governance era. (Dunleavy et al. 2006) However, even technology meets its limits when it comes to dealing with those personal matters that do not conform to the letter of the law, when compassion should be expressed or when a personal judgment call is required.

Therefore, human contact, emotional connection, and intellectual ability are still essential in order to provide a good and reliable public service. It is the role of the public servants to express sensibility and adjust the policy to individual needs, while maintaining public policies that "have their origins in the political process". (Lipsky 1980) Clearly, not all individualized cases or special demands could be met, since public servants must also maintain their obligation of equal service to all. However, this paradox is part of the daily routine of public servants as they are tasked with tastefully balancing between accommodating one's needs and maintaining the general interest.

Tasteful public service is also one that resolves complex issues creatively. It all comes down to applying the human intellectual ability and emotional sensibility to find creative solutions to conflicting interests and leading towards a "win-win" situation. While this result is not always achievable, it should always be the goal of public servants meeting difficult cases.

Application of tasteful behavior in the public service calls for "Emotional intelligence". According to Salovey and Mayer (1990), emotional intelligence is "the ability to monitor one's own and others' feelings and emotions, to discriminate among them and to use this information to guide one's thinking and actions". In other words, it is the combination of cognitive awareness and social sensibility, allowing the individual to "read between the lines" and merge rationalized tactics with social and psychological considerations.

Applied in the public servants' sphere, this signifies upholding laws and regulations, while at the same time remaining sensitive to the needs or requirements emerging from the public; applying existing regulations in the manner best-suited to the needs of the public. This is not an easy task as regulations are often rigid, not allowing room for further interpretation or a large implementation. According to Lipsky (1980), this is most challenging for those "Street-Level bureaucrats" who are dealing directly with the public while possessing more or less discretionary judgment faculties. These are the doctors, teachers, police officers, social workers, and others whose decisions shape public policies no less than the decision-makers themselves, often distant from the practical needs of the public.

Those street-level bureaucrats are tasked with bridging between the world of theory in public policy and the world of practice. In the eyes of the public, those street-level bureaucrats are judged as both the decision-makers and the implementers, when in practice they only have a certain level of discretionary faculty over the policies they ought to implement.

Those street-level bureaucrats are required to maintain a fine line between following a rigid script dictated by the letter of the law and the need to be compassionate, merging their professional and intellectual capacity with their emotional intelligence in order to be creative and treat each citizen in a tailor-made manner.

This does not go to say that tasteful behavior equals bending the law in favor of individualized cases. It does signify, however, the ability to make a judgment call, prioritize, or make an executive decision on behalf of public servants. Ingram and Schneider (1990) acknowledge the added value implementers may have, which depends on the level of discretion they express and changes they make in the core elements of the policy. This level of discretion varies according to the typology of laws, varying from the "Strong Statue approach", leaving limited if any room for implementers' discretionary judgment, to the "Support Building approach", where the decision-makers define the content while leaving it to the implementers to bring forward the how.

Adding to Ingram and Schneider's approach, we would argue that it is not only the level of discretion left for the implementers that matters, but also, and maybe mainly, the way they act in the given level of discretion they possess. Whatever the level of leverage for the public servant's discretionary judgment, the policy in place should be applied with good taste, thus in a sensible manner taking into consideration both the actual needs of the public and the original intention of the legislator.

By doing so, one should also acknowledge the risk of allowing flexibility and discretionary judgment to public servants. Issues such as inequality between citizens may arise, inconsistent with the intention of the legislator, or contradictory decisions made by implementers. (Ackroyd, Hughes, and Soothill 1989; Hupe and Hill 2007; Meyers and Vorsanger 2007) To remedy this, a codification process should be put in place, allowing direct communication and constant learning for all public servants treating similar issues. Such codification would permit public servants to remain consistent with each other's decisions, and open relevant issues for inner discussion prior to making a discretionary judgment. In referring back to our ethical analysis of the sense of smell, the public administration must be able to retrieve and re-apply past decisions and learn from past experiences. Thus, every new approach or a new judgment call made by a public servant must be codified and should be able to be retrieved if needed for future reference.

We would conclude this point by emphasizing that, in our view, public servants should be authorized to express their personal "taste": thus, use discretionary judgment and interpret the law in its largest sense possible. While admittedly this might bring about challenges and must be implemented with caution, it might also create an interdisciplinary environment and keep the public service in line with rising needs of the public in changing times. The flexibility of the public service would also facilitate a greater trust on behalf of the public in the administrative institutions, as these would manifest greater interest in coming towards the public and responding to their actual needs.

Taste, both in its physical and symbolic senses, differs from one person to another. One's appreciation of a tasteful sight, food, or action might and frequently does differ from another's appreciation of the same object. Translated onto the public sector, this would lead us to question whether a unified standard of a tasteful behavior is at all possible or would such behavior vary from one public servant to another. Asked in a different manner: Is providing a tasteful public service an innate or an acquired ability? Could one learn how to become a tasteful decision-maker in the public sphere, or is it only those born with a certain level of sensitivity and high moral grounds who can take public servant positions?

To this we would argue that just like the sense of taste itself, which starts evolving even before we are born and mainly during the first years of one's life (Savage, Fisher, and Birch 2007), tasteful behavior at its source is a born ability and each individual possesses an inherent level of taste sensibility.

However, this does not go to say that tasteful behavior cannot be taught. On the contrary, public servants, regardless of their inherent level of ethics or tasteful behavior, should learn how to manifest greater sensibility to the people they serve, how to take careful considerations before making a decision that affects the well-being of other people, and how to search for the greater good in their everyday actions. A good taste is an educated taste; it is informed, experienced, and developed.

Therefore, while some people might have greater inherent sensibility than others, the notion and practice of tasteful behavior in the public sphere are critical and must be taught as part of the public servants' professional training. Cultivating taste in the public service can either be done in the form of codification, as mentioned, or by a joint training of all those joining the public service in a given period of time, followed by a specific training dealing with the particular challenges of any given public organization. All public servants should adhere to the basic notions and ethical standards of respect, equality, the obligation to uphold the law, promote the public interest, etc.

Another scheme would be to create a clear hierarchical chain of command, used specifically for situations that call for a discretionary judgment and an ethical decision-making process. Judgments that exceed the letter of the law should not be made lightly and thus should not be made by inexperienced or unqualified public servants. A hierarchical scheme would avoid such scenarios and would allow exceptional cases to be treated by senior and specially qualified staff, who would be authorized to make a sensible and tasteful discretionary judgment in order to provide the public service required.

Moreover, a high level of tasteful public service can be maintained over time with peer-learning and continuous inner-communication allowing public servants to share and learn from others dealing with ethical questions in the workplace. While different public organizations face different ethical questions, it is also important to allow public servants from different types of organizations to learn from one another and gather around ethical questions that arise. Thus, we would call for a horizontal as well as a diagonal line of peer-learning aimed at better educating public servants to act tastefully in order to provide the most adequate public service.

Bibliography

Ackroyd, Stephen, John A. Hughes, and Keith Soothill. 1989. "Public Sector Services and Their Management." *Journal of Management Studies* 26.6:603–19.

Anker, Suzanne. 2012. "CFP: Molecular Cuisine: The Politics of Taste." New York: School of Visual Arts, October 19–21, 2012. *H-ArtHist* 5 May 2012. http://arthist. net/archive/3219 (2015.09.05).

Burke, Edmund. 1767. "On Taste: Introductory Discourse." In *A Philosophical Enquiry into the Origin of Our Ideas of the Sublime and Beautiful*, 5th ed., edited by Edmund Burke, 374–84. Pall Mall: J. Dodsley Publisher.

Denhardt, Robert B., and Janet Vinzant Denhardt. 2000. "The New Public Service: Serving Rather Than Steering." *Public Administration Review* 60.6:549–59.

Dilton, Robin S., ed. 1995. *Dignity, Character, and Self-Respect.* New York: Routledge.

DiMaggio, Paul. 1997. "Culture and Cognition." *Annual Review of Sociology* 23: 263–87.

Dunleavy, Patrick, Helen Margetts, Simon Bastow, and Jane Tinkler. 2006. "New Public Management Is Dead—Long Live Digital-Era Governance." *Journal of Public Administration Research and Theory* 16.3:467–94.

Elder, Ryan S., and Aradhna Krishna. 2010. "The Effect of Advertising Copy on Sensory Thoughts and Perceived Taste." *The Journal of Consumer Research* 36.5:748–56.

Freitas da-Costa, M., Patricia Zouein, Natasha Rodrigues, Jessica Arruda, and Maria G. Vieira. 2012. "Sensory Marketing: Consumption Experience of the Brazilian in the Restaurant Industry." *International Journal of Business Strategy* 12.4:165–71.

Gans, Herbert J. 1999. *Popular Culture and High Culture: An Analysis and Evaluation of Taste.* New York: Basic Books.

Gigante, Denise. 2005a. "The Century of Taste: Shaftesbury, Hume, Burke." In *Taste: A Literary History*, edited by Denise Gigante, 47–67. New Haven, CT: Yale University Press.

———. 2005b. *Gusto: Essential Writings in Nineteenth-Century Gastronomy.* London: Routledge.

Haldane, John. 1989. "On Taste and Excellence." *Journal of Aesthetic Education* 23.2:17–20.

Harvey, Elizabeth D. 2011. "The Portal of Touch." *The American Historical Review* 116.2:385–400.

Herz, Rachel. 2007. *The Scent of Desire: Discovering Our Enigmatic Sense of Smell.* New York: William Morrow.

Hood, Christopher. 1991. "A Public Management for All Seasons." *Public Administration* 69.1:3–19.

Hupe, Peter, and Michael Hill. 2007. "Street-Level Bureaucracy and Public Accountability." *Public Administration* 85.2:279–99.

Ikeda, Kikunae. 2002. "New Seasonings." *Chemical Senses* 27.9:847–9.

Ingram, Helen, and Anne Schneider. 1990. "Improving Implementation through Framing Smarter Statutes." *Journal of Public Policy* 10.1:67–88.

Jenner, Mark S. R. 2011. "Follow Your Nose? Smell, Smelling, and Their Histories." *The American Historical Review* 116.2:335–51.

Jessup, Bertram. 1960. "Taste and Judgment in Aesthetic Experience." *The Journal of Aesthetics and Art Criticism* 19.1:53–9.

Kant, Immanuel. 1790/1928. *Critique of Judgment.* Translated by James Creed Meredith. Oxford: Oxford University Press.

Krishna, Aradhna, and Norbert Schwarz. 2014. "Sensory Marketing, Embodiment, and Grounded Cognition: A Review and Introduction." *Journal of Consumer Psychology* 24.2:159–68.

Lee, Leonard, Shane Frederick, and Dan Ariely. 2006. "Try It, You'll Like It: The Influence of Expectation, Consumption, and Revelation on Preferences for Beer." *Psychological Science* 17.12:1054–8.

Lewis, Carol W., and Stuart C. Gilman. 2005. *The Ethics Challenge in Public Service: A Problem-Solving Guide.* Hoboken, NJ: John Wiley & Sons.

Lipsky, Michael. 1980. *Street-Level Bureaucracy: Dilemmas of the Individual in Public Services*. New York: Russell Sage Foundation.

Meyers, Marcia K., and Susan Vorsanger. 2007. "Street-Level Bureaucrats and the Implementation of Public Policy." In *The Handbook of Public Administration*, edited by B. Guy Peters and Jon Pierre, 153–63. London: Sage Publications Ltd.

Montagné, Prosper. 1988. *Larousse Gastronomique: The New American Edition of the World's Greatest Culinary Encyclopedia*, 2nd English ed., edited by Jennifer Harvey Lang. New York: Crown.

Nair, Jayakrishnan S. 2013. "Creating Brand Identity Using Human Senses." *Asia Pacific Journal of Research* 2.8:223–8.

Polansky, Ronald M., ed. 2007. *Aristotle's De anima* (422b10–16). Cambridge, UK: Cambridge University Press.

Raz, Joseph. 2001. *Value, Respect and Attachment*. Cambridge, UK: Cambridge University Press.

Romantshik, Olga, Richard H Porter, Vallo Tillmann, and Heili Varendi. 2007. "Preliminary Evidence of a Sensitive Period for Olfactory Learning by Human Newborns." *Acta Pædiatrica* 96.3:372–6.

Salovey, Peter, and John D. Mayer. 1990. "Emotional Intelligence." *Imagination, Cognition and Personality* 9.3:185–211.

Savage, Jennifer S., Jennifer Orlet Fisher, and Leann L. Birch. 2007. "Parental Influence on Eating Behavior: Conception to Adolescence." *The Journal of Law, Medicine & Ethics* 35.1:22.

Stevens, Betsy. 1999. "Communicating Ethical Values: A Study of Employee Perceptions." *Journal of Business Ethics* 20.2:113–20.

Trubek, Amy T. 2008. *The Taste of Place: A Cultural Journey into Terror*. Berkeley, CA: University of California Press.

Varendi, Heili, Richard H. Porter, and Jan Winberg. 2002. "The Effect of Labor on Olfactory Exposure Learning within the First Postnatal Hour." *Behavioral Neuroscience* 116.2:206–11.

Wansink, Brian, Sea Bum Park, Steven T. Sonka, and Michelle Morganosky. 2000. "How Soy Labeling Influences Preference and Taste." *Management Review* 3:85.

Wansink, Brian, Koert van Ittersum, and James E. Painter. 2004. "How Descriptive Food Names Bias Sensory Perceptions in Restaurants." *Food Quality and Preference* 16:393–400.

Zalta, Edward N., ed. 2006. *The Stanford Encyclopedia of Philosophy*. Retrieved 27 July 2015. http://plato.stanford.edu/

10 Making Sense of the American Society for Public Administration (ASPA) Code

In the previous chapters of this book we introduced sensory-based ethics as a new approach to improve and guide ethical conduct in the Public Administration. It is suggested that the textuality of defining rules and principles as entrenched in the Code of Ethics may extend to the sensory patterns of wisdom employed in the relationships among members of the public service professional community and policy stakeholders. We argue that sense-making highlights how the five human senses, i.e., sight, smell, hearing, touch, and taste, intersect with ethical discourse—thus compelling reflexive forms of somatic work by which a bond can be created between them and public administrators' professional practice.

Conflicting public duties are inherent in serving as a public administrator. A public servant holds direct responsibility for the welfare of the public, responsibility towards a political superior in executing public policies, as well as to his professional association. (Cooper and Menzel 2013; Lewis and Gilman 2012; Svara 2007) This, without mentioning conflicting duties related to political considerations. Competing duties or interests that emerge in the public service context can interfere with public administrators' judgment of ethical standards, thus Ethics Management becomes essential. Management of ethics comprises shared values, beliefs, and expectations of members of an organization about how the organization prevents them from behaving unethically and encourages them to behave ethically.

In an effort to ensure the professional and ethical conduct of public servants, the American Society for Public Administration (ASPA) has established its Code of Ethics. This code presents a unified ethical standard expected of all professionals in the public sector, regardless of their field of work. (Svara 2014; Svara and Terry 2009) Although, as seen previously, existing literature addresses the effectiveness of codes of ethics, fewer works deal with how these codes should be effectively communicated to its professional community. (Ireni-Saban 2015; Van Wart 2003) In an attempt to showcase how the five senses can and should be used in the practical realm of the Public Administration, we have chosen to focus on the ASPA Code of Ethics and implement its core principles in a sensory manner.

This exercise relies on the basic understanding that codes of ethics remain a vital tool for the upholding of ethical conduct in the Public Administration and in various other settings such as the private and non-profit sectors (Kidwell 2001), yet an insufficient one. While the codes provide an important setting for the acknowledgment of ethical values and define the terms for discussions related to ethical issues, most importantly, their mere existence may assist in elevating the public trust in the public organization, although they do not always allow for a practical implementation of ethical values. However, keeping the framework of the code of ethics, while implementing its values through a hermeneutic approach using the natural senses of the human being, might enable public servants to internalize the ethical values portrayed by the code and eventually provide the public with a better, more personalized, public service.

Applying Hermeneutics through Sense-Making in Public Administration Ethics

In order to allow public administrators to provide the holistic ethical public service expected of them, we suggest a hermeneutic-based Sensory model of public service. We argue that the role of sensory experience in ethical decision-making entails "somatic work", which involves the human senses of an individual that affect his perception, judgment, and behavior. (Krishna 2012; Waskul and Vannini 2008)

The suggested model is based on the belief that for a public servant to reach the most appropriate ethical decision, he or she must rely on their natural human senses and engage in "somatic work" while employing the written code of conduct. This shows that what is considered to be reflexive and natural behavior, such as the instantaneous reaction of the senses, can transcend beyond the personal sphere onto the public sphere. Sensory judgments are value judgments that have seemingly "immediate" and potent somatic importance. For instance, odor creates normative categories that can be considered "a political vehicle or a medium for the expression of class allegiances and struggles". (Classen, Howes, and Synnott 1994, 161)

It is within this framework that we suggest a hermeneutic perception of ethics management in public administration while drawing on reflexive-somatic dimensions. In our view, public administrators should follow an integrative approach that incorporates both the codified ethical standard and the *Bildung*-based somatic work when dealing with issues of ethical matters. Public administrators have an important task to avoid numbness of the senses at all cost; their positions as public servants demand that they stay attentive to the public and apply the Code of Ethics accordingly. By doing so, doing this while using his or her senses to the fullest would, and this would be our main contribution, make sense of the Code of Ethics.

Making Sense of the ASPA Code of Ethics

For the present research, we draw on the five natural senses while implementing the ASPA Code of Ethics. We believe this exercise will allow public servants to better grasp their role. As mentioned, it is the culmination of the Objective with the Subjective that will allow reaching the ideal ethical decision-making process; this is why ASPA's code of Ethics (objective) will be interpreted using the human senses in a hermeneutic (subjective) manner.

The somatic interpretation of the senses, as done in the previous chapter, would allow us to transcend the physical meaning of the senses onto a symbolic one. As a reminder, below are the core somatic expressions of the senses when used for the interpretation of codes of ethics, as we see them:

> *Sense of Sight*—the ability to foresee, envision, and think strategically and in a flexible manner. (Sullivan and Harper 1996) From the public administration point of view, this would entail the ability to anticipate the public's needs as well as foresee implications and consequences of current and developing policies.
>
> *Sense of Hearing* refers to active listening skills, which help to internalize and better communicate with the conscious and unconscious needs of the service receivers. (Lindström 2005) In the public administration this would relate to the obligation of public administrators to remain attentive to the public and place themselves in their stead without neglecting their professional obligations.
>
> *Sense of Smell* triggers personal and institutional memory and provides a broader perspective over time, which then becomes effective in justifying the added values of public administration professionals. When first smelling a new scent, one always links it to an event, a person, an object, or even a moment in time.
>
> *Sense of Touch* refers to the ability to reach out to others and engage actively and dynamically in order to provide the best possible public service. Touch in a metaphoric manner can enhance public loyalty and trust in the public administration mechanisms. (Rodrigues, Hultén, and Brito 2011)
>
> *Sense of Taste* refers to the public administrators' responsibility to act "tastefully" and apply their own discretionary judgment when needed and appropriate, make informed evidence-based decisions, and act according to the given situation in the most professional and ethical manner. (Hupe and Hill 2007; Meyers and Vorsanger 2007)

In the next few sections we chose to analyze every category of the ASPA Code of Ethics, while suggesting a sensorial implementation based on each of the five natural senses. While this exercise may seem slightly unnatural, we believe it would allow public servants to recognize certain scenarios and moral dilemmas they have or still are faced with, suggesting an innovative and hopefully practical manner for them to deal with those scenarios.

Advance the Public Interest

Public servants should have the ability to envision the consequences, implications, and potential conflicts of interests regarding policy decisions, even when the political decision-makers are unable to do so, and predict their effects. The sighted public administrator would have a broader understanding of all those potentially impacted by a policy decision through his ability to actually "see". (Maerz 2012) In this context, the public administrator should envision all implications and foresee potential consequences of a given policy and promote the public interest, even if this overshadows the individual one.

The public interest is also manifested by the public administrator's ability to retain past situations and people and use this memory in the public's favor. This institutional and personal memory is characteristic of the sense of Smell, which allows the continuity of values and long-term capacity to advance the public interest. Developing institutional memory ensures the stability required for reforms to be optimized in terms of protecting the public interest. This is especially pertinent with regard to reforms or initiatives borrowed from the private sector, such as the New Public Management reform, which require the predominance of certain unique characteristics of the public sector, while integrating best practices from the private sector. (Brignall and Modell 2000)

The sense of Taste in this context would be interpreted as the duty to use one's judgment and professional faculty in order to promote the public interest. Public servants do not operate with total autonomy and might be placed under pressure by both their political superiors or civil stakeholders such as interest groups and the public. Therefore, it is critical that public servants apply their judgment and "good taste" when dealing with complex situations involving conflicting interests. When such conflicts are not adequately considered in the practice of public administration in favor of the public interest, those impacted by a policy decision would be more likely to suffer.

An important component of advancing the public interest is the ability to hear the public's demand and internalize it in order to make the choice best suited for the public interest. In order to identify common concerns or experiences of segments of the public, administrators must ask questions (Frederickson 1997) and, we would add, it would be no less critical for them to listen to the answer. Public administrators would mostly consider themselves as able to anticipate the public's needs and requests; however, it is crucial for them to remain open and attentive to the public, even when the answers received exceed those expected. True attentiveness would lead to policy reforms and/or adjustments in current policies to better suit the public interest.

It is also part of the public servant's role to actively prevent the public interest from being compromised, by reaching out and supporting those promoting it. This active engagement is characteristic of the sense of Touch. Citizens and other stakeholders are regarded as active agents and creators of public value. (Bingham, Nabatchi, and O'Leary 2005) Public administrators should encourage their valuable contribution in creating common public good and advancing the public interest. For citizens to experience a sense of public commitment in an effective manner they need to feel engaged and being acknowledged by representatives of the public administration. Thus, their engagement would become more consistent and would contribute greatly to the advancement of the public interest, by the public, for the public.

Uphold the Constitution and the Law

In order to fully accommodate their commitments, public servants are first and foremost tasked with carefully considering, understanding, and comprehending the law and the Constitution. Sight, in its metaphoric sense, requires of them to observe and analyze the consequences of laws and regulations in place and foresee any social, economic, or political issue that may arise. The public servant's ability to identify wrongdoings or infringements relies heavily on breaching the barrier between the visible and the invisible and between theory and practice. By foreseeing potential consequences of the law public servants may assist in upholding the constitution and the law, while further advancing their adaptability to the public needs and interests.

Smell, as a catalyst for memory, can serve as a tool for public servants in upholding the law and the Constitution. It is rather essential to learn from past experience, both in terms of accumulating institutional knowledge and personal professional experience. Public administrators' ethical training should, and in most cases does, include learning from precedents, peers, and superiors' experience as means for moving forward towards a more professional, high standard, and ethical public service. Upholding the law does not necessarily imply, however, that all existing laws and regulations must be kept. By putting the metaphoric meaning of the sense of smell to use, public servants must learn from past experience and work together with decision-makers in order to adapt current legislation to the changing times and the changing needs of the public over time.

Public administrators should also use their "taste" and employ their discretionary judgment in defense of the Constitution and the rule of law. Although some of the rules remain rigid and leave no room for interpretation, others can be interpreted or applied in multiple manners. The role of the public administrator's professional and personal judgment is only enhanced when faced with conflicting laws or with a lack of a clear rule in place. Administrators are not simply the instruments of elected officials and are not powerless to act. They should therefore make value judgments in serving the public and become advocates for the rights to equality and culturally appropriate service delivery that is stipulated in federal and state laws.

Public servants are also required to carefully consider the context of every situation they face and comply with the law accordingly and sensitively. By employing a hermeneutic method and through active listening, public administrators will become more attentive to the needs of the public, will be made more aware of emergent and unexpected needs, and will be able to attend to the requirements brought up by all stakeholders. However, public servants must not confuse such reciprocal recognition of all stakeholders' voices with their public commitment to laws and legal framework within the public service as an institution, from which their profession and raison d'être are derived.

All of the above demands that public administrators manifest active engagement and constantly reach out to the public. This is in order to inform the public and ensure all rights and obligations are respected in the name of the democratic state and that no breach of the law is acceptable. This active engagement is characteristic of the sense of Touch, which is a voluntary and active measure towards the other. The requirement to uphold the law relates also to the public administrators themselves, when they are obliged to keep to the rules and legislations in order to provide the most ethical public service. This would entail reaching out to one another, enabling an inner control within the public administration and acknowledging faults when relevant. This would promise maintaining an adequate ethical level within the public administration and would, in consequence, uphold the Constitution and the law.

Promote Democratic Participation

Public administrators are tasked with shedding light over public information, activities, and initiatives and encouraging the public to partake in them. This requires public administrators to see and be seen by the public, encouraging the public itself to see and get to know internal public process as well as be seen in the public sphere. This would be achieved by allowing full transparency of the public service, enabling it to be as accessible as possible in order to increase public participation in the democratic process. To this end, public servants should communicate information regarding policy issues or reforms through various channels, which would also assist in increasing the public trust in governmental and political institutions.

Moreover, citizens should not only be encouraged to be seen in the public sphere but also to be heard by public administrators, who are required to be attentive to the public's requests, demands, and concerns and encourage them to be expressed. It is also the public servant's responsibility to identify occasions where the public's voice is not heard, or occasions where only segments of the public are being heard, and work tirelessly to remedy it. Public servants have a responsibility to encourage the public to be heard and listen carefully to what citizens have to say, as means to advance and adjust the public service to the needs and requirements of the public.

It is important to note, however, that while encouraging the public to take a greater role in designing public policies, all public servants must act "in good taste" and employ their discretionary judgment when it comes to matter of privacy, national security, or conflicting interests. One should recall it is the task of the public administration to balance the various needs arising from the public and maintain its role as the leading decision-maker in the public sphere. Therefore, not all information should be exposed to the public, and the public administration must act responsibly and tastefully when choosing the type and scale of decisions open for the public's judgment. While encouraging citizens to reflect upon issues affecting them and their communities through various forms of deliberative process, administrators should facilitate the participants' contribution while acknowledging the sensitivity and discretion required when dealing with certain matters.

The engagement and involvement of the public in the decision-making process relies heavily on learning from past experience and on various stages of trial and error. As a relatively new endeavor in the public sphere, originating from the realm of the New Public Management, the efforts to open and facilitate access to the public administration's decision-making process is without a doubt a learning process that could only develop by experience and the lessons-learned characteristic of the sense of smell. This can be achieved by allowing access and promoting critical engagement with citizens based on past policies and learning from their implementation process and long-term consequences. Open Performance Circles, initiated by public administrators for the benefit of and with the participation of the public, could involve citizens in the evaluation of administrative procedures and services and give administrators a platform from which they can identify problems, suggestions, and critiques.

It is clear that none of this would be made possible if public administrators would not take the initiative to actively engage with the public and remove procedural barriers to the participation of all populations. (King, Feltey, and Susel 1998) Reaching out to the public and "touching" the most critical needs of the public is essential, and even more so when it comes to disadvantaged or vulnerable groups whose voices are less heard and faces are less seen. Those most frequently excluded due to age, disabilities, financial limitations, geographic distance, ideological differences, and other, are often the ones who most require the public attention in order to achieve an adequate and fulfilling citizenship. Those communities, as a consequence, are often those feeling "left behind" and excluded by those in positions of power and therefore manifest a low level of trust in the public administration. The first step in touching these populations would be to work tirelessly in order to regain their trust and re-integrating them into the public realm. This by reaching out to the public, learning directly from them the existing needs and, most importantly, expressing a genuine will to collaborate and bring them back to position of power within the public sphere.

Strengthen Social Equality

The ability to identify, see, and foresee breaches in equality between the people and bring remedy to them is essential for public administrators. As part of their training process, public servants must learn to identify and be aware of the risk of inequality and flag occasions of this sort. This ethical awareness is of primordial importance for an equal and just society. Transparent feedback that raises public administration awareness of biases could promote community or grassroots with egalitarian motives to do more to prevent the implicit bias they see around them in future decisions and actions. (e.g., Son Hing, Li, and Zanna 2002) This feedback should include stakeholders' suggestions and perspectives on how to strengthen equality and fairness. (Kim 2003; Mendoza, Gollwitzer, and Amodio 2010)

This requires an enhanced sensitivity and willingness to hear the public's concerns and demands. Public servants should ensure equal rights and opportunities to all citizens with no discrimination, allowing multiple perspectives in an environment free from any prejudice and regardless of sex, gender, race, class, ethnicity, religion, or disability. Everyone's voice should be heard in an equal manner and in equal scale as the first step in respecting the public and fulfilling the duty of providing the public with the service it requires. In order to avoid any discrimination or favoritism within the public, direct contact between the administrators and the public should be encouraged. Direct channels of interaction enabling public administration to "touch" various communities and segments of the society would be an effective tool for the public to express its concerns. It is naturally the duty of the public administration to balance these concerns and requests, which at times might be conflicting; however, equal opportunity and dedication should be given to all equally.

Moreover, all public service should be provided in a sensitive and tasteful manner, acknowledging and respecting individual differences, while enforcing equality in the face of the law. The discretion and ability of public administrators to act in accordance with their professional judgment is critical in prioritizing the various requests, even considered equally, in order to allocate resources first to where they are most needed. Another essential tool in this effort is institutional and professional memory, allowing public servants to rely on past experience and learn from past success and mistakes. In the current context, this would prevent the public administration from repeating wrongdoings and past inequalities and learn from them for the future.

Fully Inform and Advise

Transparency is central in maintaining an adequate level of ethical standards in the public administration. In order to reach the goal of transparency, the decision-making process should be as open as possible, without compromising other values such as privacy and security, both in the public administration and between it and the public. Institutional and professional memory is useful in facilitating transparency, as it allows sharing accurate and essential information amongst various branches of the public administration, as well as providing the public with the most suited and best adjusted information relative to its needs. While this task is primarily the administration's responsibility, today's technologies allow the public to contribute to it as well. Public administrations can, and often times already do, use interactive open-source platforms through which public administrators as well as the public continually capture and archive institutional public knowledge: requests, responses, guidelines, regulations, practical advise, alerts, notifications regarding issues arising in the community, etc. A joint technological platform available for both the administration and public is thus becoming a living and evolving body of useful information that is accessible for the benefit of all involved.

This being said, dealing with public information requires using one's judgment and sense of taste when providing or collecting information; knowing right from wrong, prioritizing and identifying the most crucial information needed for decision-makers. The public administrators' judgment is also critical with regard to the type of information to be made accessible, preserving sensitive and discretionary information away from the public eye and available only to the selected few concerned by the matter. Public administration should gather as vast knowledge and information as possible to make accurate assessment of service performance meaningful, in order to effectively implement policy decisions in each cultural setting. Comprehensive knowledge includes community competencies and resources, understanding the role of education, wealth, social values, customs, rules, attitudes, and behaviors in target populations.

Moreover, public servants should strive to actively reach out to professionals, decision-makers, or comparable persons locally and internationally, in order to gain the most accurate and comprehensive information possible. In the information era we live in it has become possible to remove all barriers leading to knowledge and information, and using this for ameliorating public service is a particularly important cause. The learning process within the public administration comprises shattering the traditional hierarchical scheme and allowing information to flow from all directions, be it top-down, bottom-up, or vertically within the organization. (Dunleavy et al. 2006) Other technological advancements also allow reaching out to the public in consultation regarding policy issues through Crowdsourcing. This activity, becoming more and more frequent on a small scale and developing into larger ones such as States, allows public servants to operate in a closed two-way circuit where information is constantly coming from the public and/ or decision-makers and returns to the public and/or decision-makers after being revised, enhanced, and analyzed by both. It is therefore understood that the public administration is no longer the exclusive owner of information, which can nowadays be provided in a bottom-up manner just as much as in a top-down manner.

Reaching out to the public, as mentioned above, would not be useful without the public service remaining attentive to the needs and issues arising from the public. Current and developing technologies indeed facilitate access to information arising from the public in real time; however, this would not be enough without this information being taken into account when implementing policy decisions. Public servants are equally expected to use their discretionary judgment in recommending necessary policy adjustments, identifying failures in current policies, and sharing their caveats and concerns regarding the negative impact of injustice, even if this may displease political superiors. However, being placed at the administration level and not at the policy decision-making level, it is important to note that once a policy has been adopted, public servants should abstain from making any value judgment or implementing this policy decision differently than in its intended manner. Administrative discretionary judgment is indeed important; however, it should be done within internal procedures in the public administration and at predefined points in time, while maintaining a united stance in front of the public.

Last, it is important for public servants to thoroughly investigate and identify the most useful and accurate information needed by the decision-makers in order to comply with the public interest. This means seeing above and beyond the written text and being able to comprehend policy decisions and/or laws in the effort to foresee their consequences on the public and potential conflicting interests. When a reform or a policy change is discussed, public servants should look ahead and plan a detailed policy implementation plan taking into consideration how and when changes will be launched, what resources are available and/or should be allocated, who will supervise the process, how policy evaluation will be measured, etc. Following the process of overseeing the changes and foreseeing their implications, public administrators are also tasked with seeing that those changes are communicated to the public and are being adjusted to in an adequate manner. One of the major difficulties of the public administration is the implementation process vis-à-vis the public. It is for this reason that public administrators should see that accurate and relevant information is communicated to the public in time, advising the public of the best suitable modus operandi considering the policy change. A continuous and responsible flow of information within the public administration and between the public administration and the public would maintain and can even elevate the public trust and allow better cooperation between all involved in providing public services and goods.

Demonstrate Personal Integrity

Public servants must set an example to others to be seen as role models for a high standard of conduct, both personally and professionally. As the representatives of the public administration, the behavior of public servants is constantly placed under the public's eye, hence the importance of high ethical standards. Moreover, it is within the administrators' responsibility to be able to foresee potential breaches in personal integrity, be it in their own conduct or those of other public servants. Beyond being the backbone of ethical conduct in the public administration, personal integrity is necessary for acquiring and maintaining the public trust. Public servants serve as the gatekeepers of the administration as a whole, and a potential mistrust in them by the public risks compromising this critical relationship. In order to enhance and maintain a high personal integrity level, the public service can use rewards and incentives for greater compliance with public administration principles and take pride in employees who exhibit higher ethical behavior.

However, in some cases, people in positions of power within the public sphere are tempted to engage in immoral or unethical behavior, compromising the public interest and risking their own personal career. It is therefore critical that public administrators remain constantly attentive to their surroundings, acting cautiously and wisely to avoid any sort of temptation of unethical or corrupt behavior. The most important voice, when it comes to the public administration, is the voice of the public. When in doubt, public servants should be reminded of the public interest and of the means to reach it, which will always prevail over the private interest. This is also the case with the public servant's own private interest, which is only second to the public one. When reaching high positions of power within the public administration, the public's "voice" sometimes blurs; however, it is the task of public servants to remain attentive to it at all times.

In order to distinguish between the various "voices" heard, public servants must use their sense of taste and discretionary judgment in cases of potential conflict of interest, immoral acts, lack of integrity, corruption, etc. Public administrators should act with integrity and in a reliable, responsible, and coherent manner. Such "wholeness" is essentially determined by the quality of relationships a person has, to herself as well as to other people or to organizations. (Solomon 1999, 38) "Wholeness" then develops around the commitment to recognize each other's sameness and difference as equal members of one large system.

In order to reach this "wholeness" every public servant must calculate their actions and employ personal and professional judgment when encountering potentially unethical behavior. The personal integrity of the public servant and the paths he or she chooses to take would affect their personal career; however, risk also affects the public to a certain extent. Considering the role public servants play in the community, their actions might have concrete consequences affecting the public and, therefore, they must employ discretionary judgment every step of the way and keep their personal integrity intact.

One method for avoiding unethical incidents is using the personal, professional, and institutional memory in this regard. By documenting the lessons of critical incidents or cases of ethical misbehavior from the organization's most experienced administrators, the organization can create ethical guidance. Documenting such "difficult cases" and the corrective measures taken may promote personal integrity. Such a method would assist not only the public servants themselves by preventing them from making the same mistakes their peers have made, but would also be beneficial for the public, who would not have to deal with wrongdoings in the public administration nor their consequences, which may be substantial.

Promote Ethical Organizations

Public servants are not only responsible for their own personal behavior, but are also responsible for maintaining and promoting ethical behavior within the public institutions as a whole. Thus, they are charged with actively reaching out in order to avert and notify of any risk or infringement to the ethical standard of the organization. While unethical behavior is oftentimes an individual choice, its consequences can transcend beyond the individual themselves and "touch" many others. In the case of the public administration, unethical behavior of one public servant may affect the community and, at times, the public as a whole. The various public instances should educate the public servants for ethical conduct as well as hold public servants or public organizations accountable for unethical or inappropriate behavior and seek to correct wrongdoings inside and outside of the public sector. Another crucial component in the effort to promote ethical organizations is the establishment of an easy and safe channel for reporting violations of ethical conduct within the organizations, as well as from one organization to another, without fear of any personal or professional repercussions. In addition, organizations should make sure employees know that their supervisors will take immediate action and investigate claims, should they arise, regarding ethical misconduct. (Ireni-Saban 2015)

As means to promote ethical organizational behavior, public servants must remain attentive to behaviors that represent excellence in ethical conduct or lack thereof amongst public servants and act accordingly. This is by instituting procedures and affirmative steps to encourage and support whistleblowers while attending to their concerns. Employees should be monitored periodically for their behavior during difficult ethical situations and should be encouraged to share from their values-in-action experience that demonstrates public administration values such as integrity, compassion, and commitment, or use them to highlight attitudes or practices that should be halted. By listening to values-in-action experiences, ethical values would be reinforced amongst other public servants who would, in their turn, strive for high ethical professional performance.

The promotion of ethical behavior, or the sanction against it in case of a lack of one, should be done tastefully while using one's judgment to channel the situation to the benefit of the institution and the public servants within it. While unethical behavior should be banned and excluded from the public administration, the ways and methods to deal with such situations should be well thought of in advance. This is in order to create a positive atmosphere within the organization, focusing on the positive aspect of promoting ethical conduct rather than on the negative aspect of sanctioning against unethical conduct. This is especially important considering that research has demonstrated a less favorable ethical climate in the public sphere compared to the private one. (Wittmer and Coursey 1996) Ethical conduct should become natural and instinctive for public servants, rather than the path to choose in order to avoid personal or professional sanctions. This can be achieved through annual internal surveys aimed at learning the employees' attitudes towards the organization's ethical culture, periodic training sessions regarding ethical decision-making in the public sphere, and other education programs designed to enhance ethical behavior among public organizations.

An Ethical organization nurtures a culture of ethical behavior and relies heavily on years of experience, procedures of data collection, as well as practical know-hows. Relying on past experience, characterized by the sense of smell, creates an ethical work environment upholding a zero-tolerance policy for ethical infringement. This mechanism is expected to strengthen the ethical culture of the organization and its professional identity. Similar to individual ethical conduct, the organizational one can be achieved by learning from past experience—be it positive or negative. Organizations must carefully choose their employees and educate them according to the organization's Code of Ethics, while emphasizing the importance of keeping the ethical values as well as the sanctions in case of any ethical breach. The methods and means to so do can be learned from other public organizations that have gone through a similar process in the past. The same applies to dealing with ethical breaches if and when they occur—what would be the best-suited method to deal with such a scenario? How can the organization channel this into a positive outcome, if at all? Are there any lessons to be learned from the incident at hand? Parallel public organizations have most probably already dealt with such questions and their experience is extremely valuable in avoiding potential mistakes and reaching the best possible outcome.

Advance Professional Excellence

Professional excellence can only be achieved when the organization is constantly looking ahead, seeing and considering new ways to improve itself and re-invent itself. So is the case with public institutions, which must always search for ways to provide a better, more professional, accessible, and efficient public service. In the New Public Management era the methods applied in the public sector have become closer to those of the private sector, where innovation is critical for survival. (Paulsen 2005) It is therefore necessary for all public institutions to keep looking ahead and identifying ways for them to provide the best possible public service. This can be achieved by learning from parallel institutions' experience in other democratic countries; by using a comparative approach and getting acquainted with best practices from across the world, the public administration can design the most appropriate method for the local public and organizational structure. Foreseeing the needs of the public would also assist in reaching professional excellence in the public administration; in the changing times we live in, habits and lifestyles keep evolving and thus so do the needs of the public from the administration. Public organizations that would be able to identify social trends in time and foresee their implications on the policy level would be able to provide the public with a better service, thus enhancing the public trust and strengthening the relationship between the public administration and the public itself.

Listening to the public and remaining constantly attentive to its needs would also facilitate advancing the public administration's professional excellence. Listening becomes a more complicated task once there are several voices to be heard. As mentioned above, it is the voice of the public that is of first importance when it comes to public organizations; however, the public does not always speak in one voice, nor is it the only voice to be heard. Public administrators must also take into account other stakeholders such as the political level and interest groups. In these conditions it becomes clear that public administrators should not only learn to listen but also learn to think creatively in order to answer the various stakeholders' needs and requests. This does not go to say all interests should be met, which would only emphasize the need for prioritization and discretionary judgment employed by public administrators.

Public organizations must also reach out and search for professional development and advancements in public administration. As previously discussed, the public administration, or public institutions in general, no longer hold the monopoly of information in the digital age, and therefore reaching out and "touching" the public can be done in various and most effective ways in order to promote the administration's professional excellence. Information can also be found within the public administration itself, by providing open channels for administrators' feedback and suggestions of means to improve the work of the public administration. To this we would add that professional excellence does not only rely on innovation and new work methods, but can also be achieved by relying on past experience and lessons-learned from the past used for future reference. Public administrators should be empowered to share and document their experiences and learn from their peers with regard to professional behavior in general and in ethical decision-making processes in particular, in order to improve the quality of the public service delivered.

Ethics management can be achieved not only through the establishment of codified standards, but also through professional practices in the public administration. While ethics management for public administrators gradually becomes customary, it is extremely difficult to evaluate the code of ethics' efficiency and normative effect on public administrators and, as a result, the ethical level manifested towards peers, superiors, and the public itself. A hermeneutic-somatic regard of ethics management may provide a solution to this uncertainty, as it relies on the natural senses of the human being rather than on external guidelines and institutional considerations.

Through somatic work, the public administrator is implementing the ASPA Code of Ethics while applying his or her natural senses and acknowledging the other and his/her own bias. By making use of the natural senses of the individual, the various values comprising the ASPA Code of Ethics become an inherent and, with time, spontaneous action and reaction for public administrators. A somatic implementation of the Code of Ethics adds a new dimension to the rigid set of rules it presents the public administrator with. Using the senses allows the administrator to transcend the external requirements set by the code and to fully internalize his/her ethical commitments within public administration. Such engagement, developed over ethics management trainings, enables ethical consideration to be inherent to all public servants and automatically improves the quality of the public service to the benefit of the public interest. This would potentially lead to the improvement of the public service and the professional practices in the public administration.

Bibliography

Bingham, Lisa B., Tina Nabatchi, and Rosemary O'Leary. 2005. "The New Governance: Practices and Processes for Stakeholder and Citizen Participation in the Work of Government." *Public Administration Review* 65.5:547–58.

Brignall, Stan, and Sven Modell. 2000. "An Institutional Perspective on Performance Measurement and Management in the 'New Public Sector'." *Management Accounting Research* 11.3:281–306.

Classen, Constance, David Howes, and Anthony Synnott. 1994. *Aroma: The Cultural History of Smell*. New York: Routledge.

Cooper, Terry L., and Donald Menzel, eds. 2013. *Achieving Ethical Competence for Public Service Leadership*. Armonk, NY: M. E. Sharpe.

Dunleavy, Patrick, Helen Margetts, Simon Bastow, and Jane Tinkler. 2006. "New Public Management Is Dead—Long Live Digital-Era Governance." *Journal of Public Administration Research and Theory* 16.3:467–94.

Frederickson, George H. 1997. *The Spirit of Public Administration*. San Francisco, CA: Jossey-Bass.

Hupe, Peter, and Michael Hill. 2007. "Street-Level Bureaucracy and Public Accountability." *Public Administration* 85.2:279–99.

Ireni-Saban, Liza. 2015. "Understanding the Obligations of Codes of Ethics." In *Handbook of Public Administration*, 3rd ed., edited by James Perry and Rob Christensen, 598–615. San Francisco, CA: Jossey-Bass.

Kidwell, Linda Achey. 2001. "Student Honor Codes as a Tool for Teaching Professional Ethics." *Journal of Business Ethics* 29.1:45–9.

Kim, Do-Yeong. 2003. "Voluntary Controllability of the Implicit Association Test (IAT)." *Social Psychology Quarterly* 66:83–96.

King, Cheryl Simrell, Kathryn M. Feltey, and Bridget O'Neill Susel. 1998. "The Question of Participation: Toward Authentic Public Participation in Public Administration." *Public Administration Review* 58.4:317–26.

Krishna, Aradhna. 2012. "An Integrative Review of Sensory Marketing: Engaging the Senses to Affect Perception, Judgment and Behavior." *Journal of Consumer Psychology* 22.3:332–51.

Lewis, Carol W., and Stuart C. Gilman. 2012. *The Ethics Challenge in Public Service.* San Francisco, CA: Jossey-Bass.

Lindström, Martin. 2005. *Brand Sense: How to Build Powerful Brands through Touch, Taste, Smell, Sight & Sound.* London: Kogan Page Publishers.

Maerz, John L. 2012. *A Mile in Your Shoes: The Road to Self-Actualization through Compassion.* Port Charlotte, FL: Lulu Publishers.

Mendoza, Saaid, Peter Gollwitzer, and David Amodio. 2010. "Reducing the Expression of Implicit Stereotypes: Reflexive Control through Implementation Intentions." *Personality and Social Psychology Bulletin* 36:512–23.

Meyers, Marcia K., and Susan Vorsanger. 2007. "Street-Level Bureaucrats and the Implementation of Public Policy." In *The Handbook of Public Administration*, edited by James Perry and Rob Christensen, 153–63. San Francisco, CA: Jossey-Bass.

Paulsen, Neil. 2005. "New Public Management, Innovation, and the Non-Profit Domain: New Forms of Organizing and Professional Identity." In *Organizing Innovation: New Approaches to Cultural Change and Intervention in Public Sector Organizations*, edited by Marcel Veenswijk, 15–28. Amsterdam: IOS Press.

Rodrigues, Clarinda, Bertil Hultén, and Carlos Brito. 2011. "Sensorial Brand Strategies for Value Co-Creation." *Innovative Marketing* 7.2:40–7.

Solomon, Robert C. 1999. *A Better Way to Think about Business: How Personal Integrity Leads to Corporate Success.* New York, Oxford, UK: Oxford University Press.

Son Hing, Leanne S., Winnie Li, and Mark P. Zanna. 2002. "Inducing Hypocrisy to Reduce Prejudicial Responses among Aversive Racists." *Journal of Experimental Social Psychology* 38:71–8.

Sullivan, Gordon R., and Michael V. Harper. 1996. *Hope Is Not a Method.* New York: Random House.

Svara, James H. 2007. *The Ethics Primer for Public Administrators in Government and Nonprofit Organizations.* Sudbury, MA: Jones & Bartlett Publishers.

———. 2014. "Who Are the Keepers of the Code? Articulating and Upholding Ethical Standards in the Field of Public Administration." *Public Administration Review* 74.5:561–9.

———, and Larry D. Terry II. 2009. "The Present Challenges to ASPA as an Association That Promotes Public Professionalism." *Public Administration Review* 69:1050–9.

Van Wart, Montgomery. 2003. "Codes of Ethics as Living Documents: The Case of the American Society for Public Administration: The Sources of Ethical Decision Making for Individuals in the Public Sector." *Public Integrity* 5.4:331–46.

Waskul, Dennis, and Phillip Vannini. 2008. "Smell, Odor, and Somatic Work: Sense-Making and Sensory Management." *Social Psychology Quarterly* 71:53–71.

Wittmer, Dennis, and David Coursey. 1996. "Ethical Work Climates: Comparing Top Managers in Public and Private Organizations." *Journal of Public Administration Research and Theory* 6.4:559–72.

Conclusion

In this book we have attempted to offer a new perspective for ethics management in the Public Administration. It seems the traditional approaches, relying on codified rules, regulations, and guidelines, have not yielded the results expected of them and have not managed to serve as an effective tool in the hands of public administrators struggling with ethical and moral questions. These methods all depend on the internalization by public servants of codes and guidelines that are foreign to them and might even seem disengaged from their reality. Therefore, we have turned to a different approach, looking into capabilities and faculties that are inherent to all public administrators and human beings in general, to facilitate ethics management in the public administration.

From a hermeneutic point of view, the public administration is a fertile ground. Being a platform for a multitude of interactions and perspectives, public administrators must be able to consider the voice of the other by constantly remaining aware of their one voice—thus allowing themselves to remain open to each and every interaction and putting themselves in the shoes of their interlocutor, while upholding high ethical standards and remaining committed to their role as guardians of the public interest. This is certainly not an easy task, and while it might seem clear at a glance, it proves to be extremely difficult to translate into everyday life. In the effort to facilitate both the understanding and the execution of this approach, we have chosen to base the theory presented in this oeuvre on the metaphor of sensory experiences, familiar and accessible to all human beings.

As presented by a multitude of authors, metaphors enable us to perceive and construct reality. Through linguistic expressions, metaphors borrow meaning from one concept and give it to another, enabling a different sense and a new way of understanding. Relative to the public administration, this might seem an easier and more intuitive way to comprehend ethics and appropriate ethical conduct in the public service, which could be especially effective and relevant for the dynamic and ever-changing nature of the public administration. Moreover, by using the metaphor of sensory experiences, relying on the natural and instinctive faculties of all human beings, we aim to facilitate even further the comprehension and adoption of ethical values by public servants in their everyday professional conduct in the public administration.

Seen this way and approached in a hermeneutic manner, the senses are expected to make better sense in the public administration, becoming no less than tools in the joint continuous effort for an ethical public administration, in all levels. This approach can most certainly be borrowed for other purposes, be it for the private market in order to enhance ethical conduct within the organization or for personal reasons in order to educate oneself and others to reach higher levels of ethics and integrity. We did, however, limit ourselves at this point to the public sector and, more specifically, to the public administration and "street-level bureaucrats" within it as a case study for this innovative professional strategy.

While analyzing the five human senses and interpreting them in a metaphoric manner, a very pertinent conclusion came to mind. Our senses are a moral device and are constantly being employed as such even without us noticing. In other words, the way one looks at the other, or the way one chooses to listen or touch the other in a metaphoric manner, is a subconscious moral choice that derives from one's values and cultural background and affects their every interaction and relationship. For instance, the way in which one would regard a human rights issue such as refugees or a welfare issue such as healthcare varies according to his or her moral values and the culture they have absorbed throughout the years. The same can be said regarding the way one would choose to behave and the discretionary judgment they would apply (the sense of taste) in various situations—certainly a moral decision, which is frequently instinctual and subconscious. In the public administration this relates to the way a public servant would or would not use his sense of sight to look ahead and anticipate policy repercussions, or the way he uses his auditory capacity in order to relate to another person and consider them as equal while remaining attentive to their needs and requirements.

The moral question of the senses is, as we see it, mostly individual and can vary from one person to another. However, certain components or certain moral conducts can be a product of a socialized process or a political one. The culture in which the individual has been submerged has a significant effect on their moral regard and perceptions of the world. This goes to say that citizens of Western democratic societies, upholding liberal values and who place the individual in the center, will be more inclined to "touch" their interlocutors in order to get them involved and engaged in the public sphere. This compared to totalitarian societies, where the engagement of the public is minimal and therefore where public servants would avoid any "touch" with the people. In this sense, we can relate to the moral, social, and political role of the senses, which go beyond the basic ones, in a subconscious manner.

It is obvious that such conduct exists today and has existed for a long time. However, we aim to shed some light on the use of the senses while making moral and ethical decisions. By acknowledging the use of the senses in ethical decision-making and by understanding the metaphor of sensory experiences in ethics management, one can gain a certain control over their ethical conduct and potentially ameliorate it. It is a well-known fact that acknowledging the problem is halfway to the solution, and by this book we aim to bring the literature one step closer towards understanding ethical decision-making in the public administration as a structured ethical strategy.

Can we train our senses to be more or less moral? Can one have any control over the way their senses are used in terms of ethical conduct? Ethics in the public administration has been an issue for training, workshops, guidelines, and exercise. This derives from the understanding that once a certain conduct has been learned and trained on a routine manner, it could be better used when needed in real time. However, there is very little empirical evidence as to the effectiveness of codified ethical rules and regulations. It seems the inconsistency between the theory of the Code of Ethics and the reality public servants face makes it difficult to implement the principles taught and trained in the public administration. Would sensory ethical training be any different?

One of the means to develop these senses is to create a training strategy for sensory-based ethical conduct in the public administration. Unlike Code-based training strategies, focusing on the written word and its application in real-life situations, we would call for a sensory-based strategy to sharpen public administrators' senses. This type of training would first aim to help the public administrators become conscious of the use of their senses in a routine manner, not necessarily limited to ethical issues. Once an individual becomes more conscious of his or her acts and thinking process, they can better understand their motives, and again attempt to modify their conduct if and when necessary. In this sense it would be useful for public administrators to realize the extent to which they listen carefully to the public, in what way they manage to "touch" others, or how much of their professional behavior is smell-based, i.e., based on past experience they have retained.

Once the public administrators have become conscious of their sensory-based ethical behavior, it would be possible to further sharpen their senses. The aim of sensory training would be to turn the use of the senses in ethics management into a rational activity, yet such that it is so frequently applied that it becomes intuitive. Unlike the subconscious activity of using the senses for ethical purposes, through training aimed at sharpening this use of the senses, we would strive for it to become second nature for public administrators. Conscious yet intuitive. How can an activity be trained to be intuitive? Just like with metaphors, when a certain meaning is borrowed from one concept to another, sensory strategies would borrow methods that are new to the public administration from the psychological and psych-physical domains. It is therefore that training intuition would require balancing between the use of the left-brain relative to linear and logical activities and the right-brain relative to intuition and creative thinking. (Raskin 1988) This would mean paying better and closer attention to behavioral details by putting them into writing, practicing listening amongst public administrators, getting to know all existing methods for engaging the public and bringing it closer to the decision-making process, exercising role playing in order to sharpen the visualization of the other, etc.

We find it important to note, however, that the suggested ethical training strategies do not contradict or ignore the written code or inner-organizational regulations, rather they add to them. It would indeed be beneficial to base the sensory analysis on an agreed upon and codified set of rules, which serves as guidelines for the basic ethical conduct, yet avoid constructing the entire ethical training process on a theoretical codified mechanism. The sensory strategy aims to complement the codified one; one would call for the internalization of external guidelines while the other would promote the externalization of intuitive behavior.

This individual endeavor, by becoming a habit and part of the organizational culture in the public administration, would encourage more and more public servants to become conscious of their sensorial ethical habits and would, in due course, become the norm in the public administration. We would strive for a sensory ethical decision-making process whose values might be set in codified structures, yet whose interpretation is left to each and every public servant within the public administration—a unique standard to be put in place while it is left to the individual interpretation of the public servants.

It might be easier and more comprehensible to describe the sensory strategy in the public administration when considering the lack thereof. In the absence of the ability to learn from past experience and being "thrown back" by certain situations, similar to what occurs when smelling a familiar scent, the public administration will struggle to maintain high ethical values and further advance itself for the benefit of the citizens. Another example would be the engagement on the part of the public in the decision-making process and the ability of the public administration to "touch" the public and adapt itself per its needs and desires. In the absence of these abilities public servants might act as they will and the public service as a whole might deteriorate to the level of corruption. In these conditions, it seems sensory strategies not only protect the public administration from failing but also push it to constantly get better and elevate its ethical standards.

The last and a very important point we would like to add in the study of sensory ethics, which could serve as a continuation of this work, is the use of metaphoric synesthesia in the public administration. The word synesthesia originates from the Greek language and stands for *syn*—together and *aesthesis*—perception or sensation. In other words, it refers to the experience of one or more senses as a direct cause of the experience of another sense. Cytowic describes synesthesia as: "the involuntary physical experience of a cross-model association, because the stimulation of one sensory modality causes a perception in one or more different senses." (Cytowic 1997, 30) This, viewed in a metaphoric manner, can be used in the public administration in order to enhance and promote ethical conduct.

In synesthesia one attribute of stimulus inevitably leads to the conscious experience of another stimulus. (Ward 2013) In other words, a certain sensation acts as a trigger for a different sensation, i.e., a smell that triggers a certain taste in the mouth or a certain sight which triggers a certain sound. While the physical phenomenon is still under study and may vary from one person to another, it is clear that one of its main characteristics is the sense of automaticity, when the secondary sensation is virtually an inevitable consequence of the primary one, not leaving room for individual judgment or personality-based reaction. (Ward 2013)

Synesthesia occurs in a spontaneous and involuntary manner, just like the use of the senses in the public administration and in everyday life. Much like the sensory experience, synesthesia is better understood and implemented once it becomes conscious, yet remains intuitive and natural for the person. This way, by "touching" the public and getting them engaged in the public decision-making process, the public administrator immediately becomes a better listener and very much attentive to the public needs. It is as though the use of one sense in a metaphorical manner sharpens the use of another sense. Another example would be of the public servant who is experienced and who relies on his sense of smell in the metaphoric sense in order to learn from past mistakes and benefit from the institutional memory. This same public servant will consequently be able to see for a long distance, anticipate policy implementation challenges, or potential consequences of a certain policy on the public. Once again, the metaphoric sense of smell in the public administration facilitates and enhances the use of the sense of sight.

However, considering that synesthesia is an involuntary experience, how can one encourage it or make it a repeated sensation? Also, will synesthesia in the public administration be limited to certain senses influencing others, or do all senses affect one another at the same time? Lastly, how can the public administration turn synesthesia into a collective experience, not dependent on the sensorial connotations one would make when using their senses?

These questions and more would not find their answers in this present work, but require a deeper understanding of the phenomenon of synesthesia and of its potential applications in the public administration. However, to discuss the issue briefly, ethical training based on synesthesia should focus on training public administrators to automatically "activate their senses" once an ethical issue is identified. This way, for instance, when the public's opinion is sought, the administrator will immediately proceed with actively reaching out to the public (sense of touch) while listening to their concerns (hearing) and applying his or her judgment (taste) is order to implement new policies. Another example could be a public servant who identifies an opportunity or a risk for corruption within the public administration. This will instantaneously lead him or her to notify others of the risk, making it visible to them (see) while applying their own sense of "good taste" and judgment when steering clear of the risk (taste) and making this noted within the organization for future reference, both personally and institutionally (smell).

Intensive ethical trainings, which are tailor-made for public institutions and are customized to suit the specific needs of the institution, will generate automatic ethical responses among public administrators. As a result, a new generation of public administrators will be educated who are far more aware of ethical considerations and sensitive vis-à-vis the framework of the administration as well as the public itself.

To conclude, we hope this book has contributed to the understanding of non-codified ethical values in the public administration and their interpretation through the approach of metaphoric sensory experiences. While shedding light on the matter is critical and should be encouraged, it is as important to translate this approach to the real-life public administration, serving as a tool in the hands of public administrators when dealing with important and complex ethical questions.

Bibliography

Cytowic, Richard E. 1997. "Synaesthesia: Phenomenology and Neuropsychology—A Review of Current Knowledge." In *Synaesthesia: Classic and Contemporary Readings*, edited by Simon Baron-Cohen and John E. Harrison, 17–39. Malden: Blackwell Publishing.

Raskin, Patricia J. 1988. "Decision-Making by Intuition (Part 2)." *Chemical Engineering* 95.18:154.

Ward, Jamie. 2013. "Synesthesia." *Annual Review of Psychology* 64:49–75.

Index